BUDDHIST ART
IN INDIA, CEYLON AND JAVA

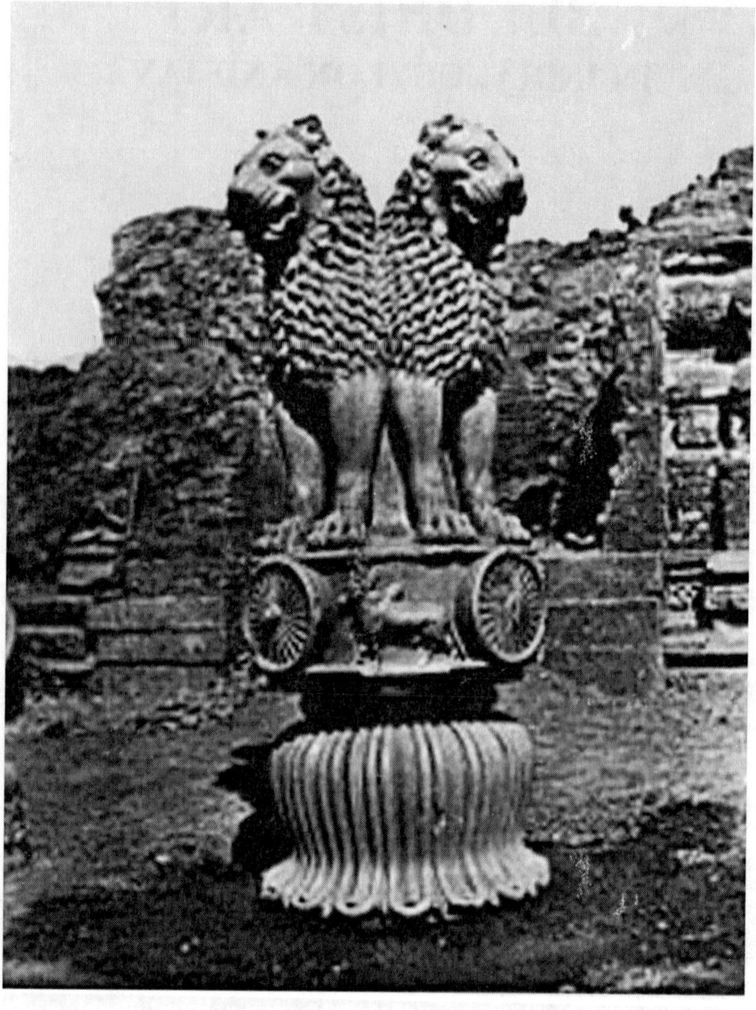

Pl.1: Lion Capital from Sārnāth, Local Museum.

BUDDHIST ART
IN INDIA, CEYLON AND JAVA

by

J.Ph. Vogel

Professor in the University of Leyden

Translated from the Dutch
by

A.J. Barnouw

Columbia University

Kaveri Books

New Delhi - 110002

Buddhist Art in India, Ceylon and Java

by J.Ph. Vogel

First Published in 1936
Edition 2022

ISBN 978-93-86463-20-3

Published by

Kaveri Books
4832/24, Ansari Road, Darya Ganj
New Delhi - 110 002 (India)
Tel.: 011-23288140, 47072321
E-mail: kaveribooks@gmail.com
web. www.kaveribooks.com

PRINTED IN INDIA

Preface

IN February 1935 the Secretary to the Delegates of the Clarendon Press addressed me regarding the possibility of bringing out an English translation of my book *De Buddhistische Kunst van Voor-Indië*, published in 1932 by Messrs. H. J. Paris, Amsterdam. He suggested at the same time that the proposed English version should include an account of the Buddhist Art of Ceylon and Java, and it was considered desirable to give special prominence to that most important monument of the Buddhist religion—the Barabudur of Java.

There was all the more reason to accept the proposal of the Clarendon Press because Dr. A. J. Barnouw, Professor of the History, Language, and Literature of the Netherlands in Columbia University, had declared his willingness to undertake the translation. Let me take this opportunity to express my indebtedness to Professor Barnouw for the care bestowed by him on this task. The readiness with which Mr. H. J. Paris has lent his co-operation is also greatly appreciated.

The inclusion of Ceylon and Java in a book dealing with the Buddhist Art of India has much to commend it. In both these islands ancient architecture and sculpture, though obviously derived from the Indian Continent, show an independent development in which the workings of indigenous sources of inspiration are unmistakable. The harmonious blending of Indian and local elements has produced in both cases a truly national art which, in my opinion, it is misleading to designate, as is sometimes done, by the slightly depreciative term 'colonial'. It may in truth be said that ancient Java especially has yielded works of art which are unsurpassed by anything found in the Indian homeland. In the Barabudur with its wonderful display of sculptural decoration the Indian *stūpa* attains its highest perfection. My brief account of this marvellous monument of the Mahāyāna is largely dependent on Professor N. J. Krom and Lieut.-Colonel Th. van Erp's volumes in which a century of archaeological research has been embodied.

In dealing with the ancient monuments of Ceylon the want of an up-to-date handbook is painfully felt. Here, too, archaeological research has made considerable progress during the last twenty years, so that earlier publications like Henry Cave's beautifully illustrated volume have now become antiquated. In my chapter on the Buddhist Art of Ceylon it has been my endeavour to include, as much as possible, the results of recent investigations. I wish here to record my great obligation to Mr. A. M. Hocart, late Archaeological Commissioner of Ceylon, and to Mr. S. Paranavitana, the learned editor of the *Epigraphia Zeylanica*, who have favoured me with many valuable suggestions.

It is, in truth, a somewhat bold undertaking to present an account of the architectural and sculptural art of Ceylon and Java in two brief chapters. But it must appear even more presumptuous to handle the Buddhist Art of all India in a book of so limited a size. That art covers a period of fifteen centuries and in the course of that vast expanse of time has revealed itself in many local schools, showing remarkably divergent varieties of style. With regard to this manifestation of Oriental Art it would certainly be most inappropriate to speak of 'the unchangeable East'.

In the present handbook it has been my chief object to give a historical outline of Indo-Buddhist Art, to sketch its various successive schools in their main characteristics, and to trace their mutual relationship. Some slight attempt has also been made to show in what manner the artistic phenomena must have followed the religious developments and spiritual movements of which they are the tangible signs.

I have preferred to keep to the firm ground of historical treatment rather than to be allured into the quicksands of aesthetic disquisition, which is too often biased by personal prejudice. At the same time I am ready to admit that in historical problems relating to Indo-Buddhist Art more uncertainty prevails than will perhaps appear from these pages. The modest size of my book did not admit of any extensive discussion of debated questions.

Perhaps these unavoidable deficiencies will be counterbalanced by the conciseness with which the main lines stand out more clearly.

Among the photographs reproduced, those relating to Indo-Buddhist Art were mostly taken by the Archaeological Survey of India, while I owe those pertaining to Ceylonese monuments to the Archaeological Commissioner in Ceylon. The photographic views and the ground-plan of the Barabudur have been borrowed, with the author's permission, from Professor Krom's book published in the same series as the original of the present volume.

J. PH. V.

LEYDEN
November 1935

Contents

List of Plates

A.S.I. = Photograph by Archaeological Survey of India.
A.S.C. = Photograph by Archaeological Survey of Ceylon.

I

Introduction

BUDDHISM has been extinct in India, the land of its birth, for nearly seven hundred years. One has to go down to Burma to find it still a vital force in the religious life of the people. But the visitor who knows Buddhist teaching through the study of the sacred writings will wonder at the spectacle of these happy Burmese folk as they go up, in festive garb, to the pagodas aglow with blazing colours. Is this cheerful religion, he will ask in surprise, the melancholy Buddhism of the ancient Pali books?

It is with equal wonder that we ask ourselves what connexion there can be between the doctrine of Buddha and the Buddhist art of India. That ancient lore weighs us down with its pessimism, it chills us with its despair of life and renunciation of the world, for it teaches man's highest aim to be release from the great sorrow which is inseparable from all existence. Such a doctrine of escape seems a barren soil for an art such as we find in India, an art which revels in luxuriant forms and profusion of colours.

It is a case of nature refusing to be regulated. The temper of the Indian people has asserted itself like sunshine breaking through the clouds. The Indian, in his inmost being, feels a powerful impulse to worship the deity and to manifest that worship in visible signs and tangible symbols.

In Buddhist India it was the person of the great Master himself which satisfied that impulse to worship. The homage of his followers raised him upon the throne of the deity, which he himself had left empty. He was at first worshipped in his relics, later on also in his image.

That deep-rooted need to adore is coupled in the Indian with yet another craving, a veritable passion for adornment, the evidences of which can still be observed in present-day India. The Hindu covers not only the white walls of his house with various colourful figures, he decks even animals, such as elephants and horses, with paints, if only their natural hue lends itself as a background for gaily tinted ornament. This pleasure in decoration, which sometimes deteriorates into a mania, also manifests itself, with ever-increasing insistence, in old Indian literature. It is, indeed, one of the most characteristic features of the plastic art of the Indians.

Those who know Buddhist art solely from the ruins, the mouldering images, the faded frescoes of India proper, can scarcely visualize the gay splendour which those ancient sanctuaries must once have radiated. Such an orgy of colours would dumbfound a Westerner. The surface of these crumbling buildings was once covered with a layer of gleaming white plaster, which was doubtless not left unadorned.

One can still find traces of colour and gilding on the sculptures of stone and stucco. Those mutilated grey stone images of Buddha must have stood there once with orange robe and gilded skin, as the faithful imagined that the Master himself had walked the earth. But one has to go to Burma, or to Ceylon, where Buddhism is still a living religion, in order fully to realize the gorgeousness of that Oriental splendour.

Though it is difficult to discover any connexion between the doctrine of Buddha and the plastic art of the Buddhists, it does not follow that this art never expresses the serene peace of mind, the infinite compassion and tenderness, and similar sublime qualities that mark the moral teaching of the Master. But the profound philosophical foundations upon which the Buddhistic world religion has been built can be left out of account when the object of our study is the wealth of sculpture and fresco that has been lavished upon the adornment of that noble edifice.

We must, however, give a moment's thought to the Buddha himself, the first person of that holy Trinity—the Buddha, the Dharma (his Doctrine), and the Sangha (his Congregation)—to whom every faithful Buddhist turns for protection. For the life of the Buddha was to the artists of ancient India an inexhaustible source of inspiration when they were called upon to decorate the sacred shrines.

This is, in brief outline, the legendary story of his

life. In the town of Kapilavastu, at the foot of the Himālayas—to be more exact, on the border of present-day Nepāl—King Śuddhodana ruled long ago over the tribe of the Śākyas. He had married a princess whose name was Māyā. One night Queen Māyā dreamt that the future Buddha—the Bodhisattva, as the Buddhists call him—descended in her womb in the shape of a white elephant. In the morning she recounted her dream to her husband. He summoned Brahman soothsayers, and these predicted that she would bear a son who was destined to become either a world-ruler or a Buddha. When the time of her confinement approached, Māyā went to the park called Lumbinī, a pleasure garden not far from Śuddhodana's capital. There she gave birth to the child who was destined to become the founder of a world religion. He was given the name of Siddhārtha. When the prince was sixteen years old he married Yaśodharā, whose hand he had won by his prowess in knightly contests. For young Siddhārtha, says the legend, was an excellent archer and an athlete skilled in many sports.

But the time approached at which Siddhārtha reached the turning-point of his life—his renunciation of the world. The story goes that his father, King Śuddhodana, was far from pleased with the prospect of his son becoming a Buddha, and tried his best to prevent it. He let the prince indulge in all the pleasures that an Indian court affords, and kept him ignorant of the sorrows of mankind. But there came to Siddhārtha four experiences that made him another being. Driving one day in his chariot he saw an old man; another time he found a diseased man; on his third ride he discovered a corpse. His charioteer, Chhandaka, revealed to him the truth that old age, sickness, and death are inseparably linked with human existence. This made him realize the vanity of worldly pleasures, and when, on a fourth excursion, he met a mendicant friar, he decided to follow his example and renounce the world.

The following night Siddhārtha left his father's palace. His wife Yaśodharā had just given birth to a son. But even the sight of his wife asleep with her new-born babe did not shake his determination. On the contrary, the sleeping servant girls, who had tried to distract him with music and dancing, aroused his disgust, and he told his charioteer to saddle his horse.

The king had ordered the city gate to be closed in order to prevent the prince's escape, but a deity opened it for him, and Yakshas supported the hoofs of the horse Kanthaka, lest the keepers should be wakened by their clatter. He rode all night and in the morning sent his servant with the horse back to town. He took off all his princely trappings, clipped his long hair, and bartered his costly robe for the simple garb of a hunter whom he met in the wilderness.

Having thus freed himself from all worldly ties, he began to study philosophy under two Brahman masters, who trained him in meditation and self-chastisement. But after six years of austere asceticism, he realized that this was not the way to illumination. He put an end to his long fasting and decided to find the Truth by independent meditation.

He sat down at the foot of the holy fig-tree. Here he withstood the onslaught of Māra, the Satan of the Buddha legend, who with his host of demons tried to oust him from his seat under the tree. He also resisted the allurements of Māra's daughters. Then at last the Truth revealed itself to him. From that moment he was the Buddha, that is, the Enlightened One. His spiritual rebirth is called Bodhi, that is Enlightenment, and the holy fig-tree, under which it occurred, is known as the Bodhi tree.[1]

After his spiritual awakening Siddhārtha, now the Buddha, departed for the holy city of Benares, which, it seems, was already, at that early period, a centre of religious life. Here, in the Deer Park outside the city, he preached, for the first time, the Truth which he had conquered with so much pain and labour. His audience consisted of the five young penitents who had been his fellow students in the school of the two Brahman philosophers. They had

[1] When the belief in numerous Buddhas had become general, the historic Buddha was designated as Śākyamuni or Śākyasiṃha, i.e. the Sage or Lion of the race of the Śākyas. He is also called Gautama.

despised him when he abandoned asceticism; now they became his first converts.

The doctrine taught by the Buddha in the Deer Park at Benares is summarized in the Four Noble Truths. They may be briefly defined as follows. All existence is inseparably linked with suffering. The cause of this suffering is desire. In order to destroy the cause of this suffering, one must shed all desire. This can be achieved by striving for good thoughts, good words, good deeds.

The dramatic part of the Buddha's life has herewith come to a close. He continued to preach his doctrine until his eightieth year, wandering around with his Order of mendicant friars, whose number steadily increased. He won also many adherents, who did not renounce the world, but who accepted the new doctrine and provided the brethren of the Order with food, clothes, and shelter.

There are a few incidents that stand out clearly in that somewhat monotonous existence of the itinerant preacher. It is especially the miracles that lend themselves to plastic presentment, and Buddhist art has often portrayed them.

The story goes that one day Buddha's wicked and envious cousin, Devadatta,—he has been called the Judas of the Buddha legend—loosed a furious elephant against him; but as soon as Buddha touched the animal, it quieted down.

Another time Buddha's thirst was quenched in the

wilderness by a monkey with a pot of palm wine. After that laudable deed the monkey, not wishing to live any longer, drowned himself in a well, but he was rewarded by his immediate rebirth in heaven.

Buddha died in his eightieth year, or, to use the phrase of the Buddhist texts, he passed into Nirvāna. His death occurred at Kusinārā, an out-of-the-way little town not otherwise known in the history of India. Thither he went with his disciples, and there he lay down to die.

According to Buddhist tradition the Buddha's Nirvāna took place about the year 480 before our Christian era. The Buddha's passing is described in detail in a famous work entitled *Mahāparinibbāṇa-sutta*, which is written in Pali, the sacred language of the southern Buddhists.[1]

The Book of the Great Nirvāṇa recounts conversations which the Buddha held with his disciples shortly before he passed away. These contain two passages which are of special importance for the genesis of Buddhist art. Buddha is said to have directed his disciples to bury his remains under a tumulus, a so-called *stūpa*, the traditional sepulchre of worldly monarchs. And he further ordered that after his death the faithful should visit especially those four places which were linked with the chief events of his life. These are the garden called Lum-

[1] Translated into English under the title *The Book of the Great Decease* (*Sacred Books of the East*, vol. xi).

binī near Kapilavastu, where he was born; the holy fig-tree of Bodh Gayā, where he had found the Truth; the Deer Park near Benares, where he had first preached his doctrine; and the Sāl Grove of Kusinārā, where he had passed into Nirvāṇa. It is questionable whether these two commandments were actually given by Buddha himself. But their authenticity is immaterial to our purpose. So much is certain that obedience to those commandments gave the first impetus to the rise of Buddhist art.

II

The Monuments of Aśoka (250 B.C.) and the National School of Sculpture of Central India (150—50 B.C.)

ACCORDING to sacred tradition eight *stūpas* were erected over the Buddha's remains immediately after his death. We cannot form an adequate conception of these monumental reliquaries, for not a trace of them has been discovered. We may assume, however, that they were the prototypes of the numberless *stūpas* that were subsequently raised all over the Buddhist world, the type attaining its highest perfection in the Barabudur.

The history of Buddhist art does not really commence until the reign of the great Aśoka, *c.* 250 B.C., two centuries and a quarter after Buddha's Nirvāna. It is clear from his inscriptions on rocks and on pillars that the first great monuments owed their origin to the religious zeal of the emperor who ruled over the whole of Āryāvarta[1]. These columns, erected as bearers of Aśoka's pious edicts, are smooth and beautifully polished monoliths with grooved capitals which are surmounted by the image of some animal. The abacus, as a rule, is also decorated with animal and floral ornaments.

It is surprising that this art, at its inception,

[1] Āryan India, i.e. India to the north of the Vindhya Range.

created monuments of such perfect beauty. The monarchs of the Maurya dynasty, to which Aśoka belonged, are known to have entertained political relations with the Seleucids. Aśoka probably had his memorial columns executed by Graeco-Syrian sculptors, who, through agelong tradition, were experts in the carving of stone. This assumption is supported by the enormous lion capital (Plate 1) which was excavated in 1904 at Sārnāth near Benares. It once surmounted a column upon which Aśoka had an edict against the schismatics engraved. It is impossible to say at what time and by what vandals this impressive monument was destroyed. The capital was badly damaged by its fall from the high column. It bears four half-figures of stately lions which once supported a stone wheel or *dharmachakra*, the symbol of the Law that Buddha had proclaimed. The abacus is decorated with four effigies of the Sacred Wheel alternating with four animals—an elephant, a bull, a horse, and a lion. In all probability these animals symbolize the Four Quarters, the whole monument being meant to convey that the Good Doctrine was destined to spread in all directions to the ends of the earth.[1] No more suitable place for such a monument could have been found than the Deer Park of Benares, where the

[1] In votive inscriptions the Buddhist Community is usually defined by the adjective *chāturdiśa* meaning 'belonging to the Four Quarters, universal'.

12 *Monuments of Aśoka (250 B.C.) and the National*

Buddha had first proclaimed his doctrine or—in Buddhist phraseology—had set going the Wheel of the Law.

Aśoka is said to have erected also many *stūpas*—tradition even fixes their number at 84,000!—and, in connexion with these, he built, no doubt, many monasteries and convents. But not a single one of these structures has been preserved in unmistakable condition.

In its earliest form we know the *stūpa* from the Sānchi mound in Central India. Its summit bears three such monuments. The *stūpa* proper is a massive hemisphere surrounded by a circular terrace and crowned with a square railing of stone, which must once have enclosed a standard supporting a parasol (Plate 4). It is a primitive type of building, a sort of masonry tumulus intended as a receptacle for relics. Its artistic value is but slight.

The great *stūpa* of Sānchi is surrounded by a high stone railing to which, probably about the middle of the first century B.C., four monumental gates were added. These so-called *toranas*, of a very peculiar construction, are entirely covered with sculpture, very remarkable specimens of genuine Indian art (Plate 5).

The same ancient technique, in somewhat more primitive form, is found at Bharhut, also in Central India. Here stood at one time a *stūpa* which was also enclosed within a high massive balustrade of stone with gates of similar construction.[1] In its general character the sculpture of Bharhut is essentially identical with that of Sānchi, and yet in certain respects the two differ profoundly.

In this connexion a third monument claims our attention—the stone balustrade that encloses the Temple of the Mahābodhi, or The Great Enlightenment, at Bodh Gayā. It was formerly erroneously called the Aśoka railing; from votive inscriptions it is evident that it must be attributed to the Śunga dynasty which succeeded the Mauryas in northern India.

At Bharhut some of the pillars are decorated with male and female figures as guardians of the entrances to the sanctuary. They are remarkable on account of their archaic character. The male gate-keepers, whom the inscriptions state to be Yakshas and other minor deities, are symmetrical in build, rigid of attitude, and forbidding of countenance. Their female counterparts are more graceful (Plate 2) and usually seize with outstretched hand the branch of a blossoming tree above their heads.

The sculptured decoration further consists of panels in which scenes are portrayed from the life of the Buddha. But the Bharhut sculptors were still

[1] The *stūpa* and sections of the balustrade have fallen a prey to rapacious villagers, but Sir Alexander Cunningham has saved a large part of the eastern gate and fragments of the railing. They have been reconstructed and are now on view in the Indian Museum at Calcutta.

fonder of the stories concerning Buddha's previous existences, especially of those in which he appeared on earth in the shape of some animal. These popular fables, called *jātakas*, are illustrated in profusion both on the stone railing-pillars and along the coping of the large balustrade.

The Bharhut sculptors, it would seem, did not trust their own skill in illustrating the sacred stories. They thought it advisable, at any rate, to provide their reliefs with explanatory legends. Both the Bharhut and the Sānchi monuments contain, besides, numerous inscriptions which mention the names of the various persons who each had a section of the balustrade made. From these records it is clear that such a monument resulted from the co-operation of a large number of members of the Buddhist community.

The sculptors of the Sānchi gates also drew their inspiration from the wealth of Buddha legend and the *jātakas*, but their work reveals a more developed understanding of composition and perspective and a greater skill in the rendering of the sacred stories. The most striking feature of the Sānchi sculptor's art is his loving attention to detail.

Sometimes the artist reproduces a consecutive story in one and the same bas-relief by portraying the dramatis personae twice or three times in the various episodes in which they act their parts. A similar synoptic method of illustration is found also in the Christian art of the Middle Ages.

One other peculiarity is common to the art of Bharhut and Sānchi. They avoid the portrayal of the Buddha. Not only images of the Buddha are entirely absent from this earliest phase of Buddhist art, but even in the numerous reliefs which refer to the legend of the life his presence is always indicated by some symbol—a footprint, a vacant throne, or the sacred Bodhi tree under which he attained supreme wisdom.[1]

A relief belonging to the central architrave of the east gate at Sānchi proves that the sculptors also avoided the portrayal of Śākyamuni in that period of his life prior to the Bodhi, in which he is indicated by the name of Bodhisattva. It represents the Great Departure from Kapilavastu (Plate 6*a*). On the left is the walled city with balconies full of spectators. The horse, which appears five times, is the steed Kanthaka which carried the prince on the flight from his father's palace. But the prince himself, i.e. the Bodhisattva, is not shown. His presence, indeed, is indicated by the parasol, the royal emblem, which a servant holds up above the head of the invisible rider. After the horse has passed the city gate, we see it, three times in succession, on its way to the spot where the Bodhisattva dismounts in order to begin a hermit's life in the wilderness. This place

[1] The four principal events of Buddha's life are also represented by symbols: his miraculous birth by a lotus-flower, his spiritual awakening by the Bodhi tree, his first preaching by the Wheel of the Law, and his death by a *stūpa*.

is symbolized by the two footprints marked with a wheel, and before which the faithful Chhandaka is kneeling down. The horse Kanthaka, with its keepers, thereupon returns towards the palace, but now it is actually a horse without its rider and the parasol has accordingly been omitted. But it appears, instead, above the two footprints so as to emphasize the presence of the Bodhisattva.

The synoptic method of illustration is again applied in the relief of the south gate representing the Shaddanta-jātaka, which is also portrayed on the western gate. The 'six-tusked' elephant who, as Bodhisattva, is the hero of the story, is first seen bathing in the lotus pond and next approaching with stately step the fatal ambush where the hunter lies in wait for him (Plate 6*b*). The most striking feature of this relief is the skilful composition of the herd of elephants. The banian tree with its drooping roots is also exquisitely characterized. It is this loving observation and careful reproduction of nature which mark the sculpture of Sānchi as one of the highest expressions of Indian art.[1]

By the side of the Sānchi elephants the medallion of Bharhut which illustrates the *jātaka* of the *ruru* deer is distinctly primitive in treatment (Plate 3). But its manner of presentment is nevertheless the same. Here also the entire story is enacted within the frame of one panel. In the foreground is shown

[1] Cf. Marshall, *Guide to Sānchi*, pp. 74 ff.

how the noble deer—the Bodhisattva himself—rescues the young merchant from the river raging in flood. The merchant is shown again betraying, ungrateful wretch that he is, to the hunt-loving king the deer that has saved him. The king is aiming his arrow at the deer where it lies resting under a tree. But he does not shoot; he repents, and stands with devoutly folded hands before the deer, while the betrayer, shown a third time, seems to hide himself in shame behind his back.

These few examples may suffice to help us understand the ancient art of Bharhut and Sānchi in its characteristic features. In spite, or perhaps on account, of its primitive character this art possesses a powerful charm by virtue of its genuine *naïveté*, its great love of nature, and, pre-eminently, its devotion to and intense veneration of the Buddha. That veneration manifests itself beyond all doubt in the scrupulous avoidance of his portrayal in visible form.

III

The Graeco-Buddhist Art of Gandhāra
(50 B.C.—A.D. 500)

THE expansion of Buddhism over all India was chiefly due to the religious zeal of the Emperor Aśoka. Gandhāra, the border province in the farthest north-west which is cut off by the Indus from the Land of the Five Rivers (Panjāb), is mentioned among the countries that were converted to the Good Law. It was from Gandhāra that Buddhism, at the beginning of our Christian era, started on its triumphal progress across central Asia to the Far East.

This part of India was ruled in the second and first centuries B.C. by princes of Hellenic name and culture. Their homeland was Bactria, but they had extended their power over present-day Afghānistān and over those Indian provinces that had once formed part of the empire of the Achaemenids. When attacks from Parthians and Scyths began to press them hard in their homeland, they removed the centre of their realm from Bactria to India. One of them, Menander, figures as a zealous Buddhist in a well-known Pali document entitled *Milindapañha*, or 'The Questions of Milinda'.

Thus it happened that in Gandhāra Buddhist faith and Greek culture met and mingled, resulting in that peculiar hybrid art which is called Graeco-

Buddhist. It occurs also in the adjoining mountain regions, in Afghānistān and in the city of Taxila, well-known from the Indian campaign of Alexander the Great.

Since the early nineteenth century, when the Indian borderland was opened up to scientific exploration, the monastic ruins of ancient Gandhāra (now the district of Peshāwar) have yielded an incredibly large quantity of sculptures, which have since been distributed among several museums (Calcutta, Lahore, Peshāwar).[1] On account of its pseudo-classical character this Gandhāra sculpture attracted wide attention, and experts, in their first enthusiasm, were inclined to overrate its artistic value.

Both the sacred monuments and the sculptures with which they were so lavishly decorated showed unmistakable traces of destruction. So many different conquerors have forced their way through this border-region towards the wide plains of Hindustān that it is difficult to fix the blame on any one vandal in particular. We have a clue, however, in the account of the Chinese pilgrim Hiuen-Tsiang, who travelled through Gandhāra about the year 630; he was told that a cruel king of the Huns, whose name was Mihirakula, had, a century before, ransacked and destroyed the Buddhist monasteries of that country.

[1] Collections of Graeco-Buddhist sculpture are found also in the British Museum in London, in the Museum für Völkerkunde at Berlin, and in the Louvre at Paris.

Enough is left, however, of these buildings, frequently perched upon steep rocks, to convince us that their architectural character is purely Indian and that foreign influence is noticeable only in the sculptural decoration. Here again we find the *stūpa*, repeated a hundredfold in various dimensions, as the most typical representative of Buddhist architecture. But the shape of the ancient relic-shrine has undergone a profound change. We still recognize the hemisphere, but it is loftier and more slender than that of the *stūpas* in Central India. It is, moreover, supported by a square substructure, consisting usually of several terraces, that can be ascended by one or more flights of steps. This construction lends to the whole a tapering effect, and it is not surprising to find the Chinese pilgrims describe these monuments as towers.

The stone balustrade and the *toranas* of Central India are absent. The sculptors have decorated the *stūpa* itself. Their work consists mainly of rows of reliefs which visualize the life of the Master in chronological order and with such painstaking completeness that hardly a single episode is missing. Scenes from the *jātakas*, on the other hand, are scarce. The few that do occur were taken preferably from the touching stories of Prince Viśvantara, of the King of the Śibis, and of the hermit boy Śyāma, and seldom from the naïve beast fables in which the sculptors of Bharhut and Sānchi took delight.

On closer observation we are struck by the classic symmetry and restraint of the composition, which contrasts sharply with the baffling exuberance of the Sānchi panels. The scene, as a rule, is dominated by the hero and principal character of the story, the Buddha Śākyamuni, who, standing, sitting, or lying down, occupies the centre of the panel and often exceeds the other personages in size. For here the Master's presence is no longer indicated, as it was in the older art, by means of a footprint or some other symbol.

Let us compare the presentment that Gandhāra gives of the departure from Kapilavastu (Plate 9) with the elaborate treatment of that same episode on the east gate at Sānchi (Plate 6*a*). It is a favourite theme of Graeco-Buddhist art. The Bodhisattva, as a rule, occupies the centre of the panel, riding towards us on his horse Kanthaka whose hoofs are supported by Yakshas. He is dressed, as Prince Siddhārtha, in royal garb, but the aureole around his head marks him as Bodhisattva. By his side stands a sunshade-bearer, and on the other side a warrior in a cuirass who carries a bow. This is Māra, the Indian Eros and also the Satan of the Buddhists, who vainly tries to make Buddha waver in his resolution.

Now, for the first time, we find also detached images of the Buddha wearing a simple monk's habit but marked with the visible tokens of his superhuman nature—the *ūrnā* and *ūshnīsha*[1]—as he is described in the sacred books. But this first sculptural representation of the Buddha betrays, at the same time, its half-foreign origin by the folds of the drapery, by the nimbus round the head, and by the Buddha's features which sometimes remind one of Apollo or Dionysus.

The appearance of the Buddha image was an event of the utmost importance. Previously the *stūpa* had been the sole object of worship. Now the image of the Buddha claimed part of the believer's devotion. For the Master did not figure exclusively in episodes from his legend; it was only natural that the artists should have gone one step farther and pictured him all by himself. But these solitary Buddhas are always shown in relief, never as statues carved in the round.

There is little uniformity of style. The treatment of the head especially exhibits considerable variety. Sometimes it reminds one of the ideal type of classical art, and then again one finds a more realistic Hindu type, occasionally even provided with a moustache (Plate 7). The hair is sometimes tied into a graceful krobulos, but just as often, in accordance with the canon, the head is covered with short curls that are twisted to the right. The latter

[1] The *ūrnā* is a slight eminence of circular shape between the eyebrows, often indicated by a jewel or a piece of crystal. The *ūshnīsha* is the well-known knob on the top of the head, which in later Buddha images is often given a tapering shape.

treatment has remained in vogue in later Buddhist art. These variations were doubtless due to the clash between aesthetics and orthodoxy. The gesture of the hand, however, became fixed at an early stage. The right hand, as a rule, is raised to the height of the shoulder, the open palm being turned towards the spectator as expressive of the Master's grant of protection (*abhaya*).

It was, no doubt, reverent scruple that for centuries kept the faithful from portraying the Buddha, but by this time all trace of it had vanished. Innumerable Buddhas of stone or stucco, and sometimes of supernatural size, were placed in the monastery cells or arrayed in uniform rows along the walls of the convent courts. The Buddha image, soon after its appearance on the scene, is even turned into a decorative motif, to be applied in profusion upon the square basements of the *stūpas*.

Besides these unadorned Buddha statues the monasteries of Gandhāra have yielded numerous images that represent a young man in princely garb (Plate 8). These gallant figures, when they were first discovered, were supposed to represent the Master before he became Buddha. This interpretation is doubtless correct in so far as they were originally intended as images of Prince Siddhārtha. For he is represented in exactly the same manner in the reliefs that visualize the Buddha's worldly existence. There are cases, however, in which this explanation does not hold. We sometimes find a seated Buddha placed between two such princely figures, a grouping which becomes typical of all later Buddhist art. It is clear that in such a case the attendant figures are celestial Bodhisattvas, those ethereal evaporations from the first terrestrial Bodhisattva[1] whose number had grown to a countless multitude. It is even possible to recognize a few outstanding figures among that uniform host, in the first place the future saviour Maitreya, who holds an ambrosia vase in his right hand, perhaps also Avalokiteśvara, recognizable by his attribute the red lotus-flower, who inspires such profound veneration in the later Buddhist world. Thus we find, in this Graeco-Buddhist art, the beginnings of the Mahāyāna, which lays special emphasis upon the cult of the Bodhisattvas.

All attempts to define the period in which this remarkable art flourished have foundered on insurmountable difficulties. Inscribed sculptures are few, and fewer still are those that give a date. The Buddha of Loriyān Tangai is dated in the year 318, and the so-called Hashtnagar pedestal bears the date 384. But since it is not certain which era has been used, these inscriptions do not offer any definite clue.

It is tempting to ascribe the origin of Graeco-Buddhist art to Greek princes such as Menander

[1] That is to say, the being which, having been born as Prince Siddhārtha, was predestined to become the Buddha Śākyamuni.

(*c.* 150 B.C.), whose coins still testify to their rule over these regions. But the evidence supplied by the coins that have come to light points rather to the reign of the Scythian Prince Azes as the period in which, most probably, this art had its beginning. Azes reigned about half a century before the Christian era, at a time when north-western India had been wrested from its Greek rulers by the same conquerors who previously had ousted them from Bactria.

This much is certain that the heyday of Gandhāran Buddhism occurred during the reign of yet a new race of foreign conquerors, who about A.D. 50 subdued northern India and made the satraps of Parthian and Scythian blood their tributaries. These were the Yue-chi, whose destinies can be traced, with the aid of Chinese records, beginning from the time when they wandered away from their homeland in central Asia. Under the dynasty of the Kushānas they founded a realm that must have encompassed northern India, Afghānistān, and Bactria. It reached the summit of its power under the rule of King Kanishka, whom we find described as a mighty warrior but also as a powerful patron of Buddhism. Outside the walls of Purushapura (Peshāwar), the capital of Gandhāra, he founded a *stūpa* which is praised by the Chinese pilgrims as the largest pagoda of India. Remains of this sanctuary were discovered in 1908, as well as a bronze relic-casket on which the king is portrayed in his foreign garb. This small receptacle is an invaluable document for the history of Graeco-Buddhist art. That it actually belongs to that school is proved by the peculiar mixture of Indian and Hellenistic motifs (Buddha, garland-bearers, and geese) with which it is decorated. But the clumsy execution seems to indicate that the school of Gandhāra at that time was on the decline. Royal patronage evidently stimulated production, but the large output leaves the impression that under the rule of King Kanishka, supposedly in the early second century of our era, the power of plastic rendering was on the wane.

The school of Gandhāra seems to have lingered or for a few hundred years, but the destruction of the monasteries in the sixth century by Mihirakula, King of the Huns, was a disaster from which it never recovered.

In appraising the artistic value of this hybrid sculpture we must take into account the course of development that has been sketched so far. The Graeco-Bactrian artists distinguished themselves at the outset by a remarkable creative power. They portrayed the entire life-story of the Buddha in plastic forms, which in many an instance set a tradition both in India and beyond that lasted as long as Buddhist art survived. In contrast with the symbolism of the national school of Central India, they

[1] Of contemporary painting not a trace has survived.

preferred direct representation, and applied it with so much talent that the various episodes, in spite of the disarrangement and mutilation of the reliefs, can in most cases be definitely identified. The painstaking workmanship bestowed on some of these reliefs reveals the artistic sense and pious mood of the sculptors.

On the other hand, it must be admitted that Gandhāra, for all its output, has produced few works of art of outstanding merit. Among those few we feel tempted to include the remarkable image from the neighbourhood of Peshāwar which represents a king of the Yakshas. The Buddha emaciated by his long fast, for which the sculptor seems to have drawn his inspiration from the *Padhāna-sutta* of the *Suttanipāta*, must also be prized as a work of great significance and gripping realism, although in the later art of India it never stimulated imitation. Similar realism marks the striking scene of Māra's threatening host of demons on the march to wrest from the Buddha his seat under the Bodhi tree.

The bulk of Graeco-Buddhist sculpture, however, is marred by a slovenly coarseness resulting from the mechanical repetition of existing motifs. Enthusiastic admirers of Indian art are apt to deplore, or even to execrate, the intrusion of a foreign influence. But we have to accept it as an historical fact of which we can neither deny the existence nor minimize the significance.

IV

The Sculpture of Mathurā under the Kushāna Dynasty (A.D. 50—200)

MATHURĀ, which is now the focus of the cult of Krishna, the divine shepherd, must, in the olden days, have been one of the strongholds of Buddhism. It owed its importance as an emporium to its situation on the great trade-route which connected the two capitals of the north-western border-province, Pushkalāvatī [1] and Taxila, on the one side with Pātalīputra on the lower Ganges and on the other with Bharukachchha,[2] the great seaport on the west coast.

Buddhism, in its gradual expansion over the Indian continent, naturally followed the great trade-routes. It is clear also, from numerous votive inscriptions, that among the merchant class its most zealous adherents were counted. Anāthapindada, the *seth* [3] of Śrāvastī who presented Buddha with the park 'Jetavana', lives on in legendary lore as the generous *upāsaka* [4] par excellence.

[1] Subsequently superseded by Purushapura, now Peshāwar.

[2] Now Broach.

[3] This word, which is etymologically identical with Sanskrit *śreshthin* (Pali *setthi*), denotes a wealthy merchant, banker, or master of a guild.

[4] *Upāsaka*, feminine *upāsikā*, is the name for those followers of Buddha who, unlike the monks and nuns, had not renounced their social position and married state.

It is not surprising, then, that during the first centuries of our era the Good Law flourished in Mathurā. Numerous pieces of sculpture that have been found both in the city and in the district of the same name bear testimony to its former ascendancy. Not one of the buildings to which they once belonged has been preserved. The great trade-route was also the highway along which the rapacious invaders from the north-west pushed on towards the wealthy cities in the plains of the Ganges. Many a time the city on the Jamnā must have been sacked and destroyed.

With the aid of the numerous inscriptions that have been found here we can form some idea of the aspect of the city under the rule of the Kushāna dynasty, when Buddhism was in its heyday at Mathurā. The walled-in city on the right bank of the Jamnā was encircled by a wreath of sanctuaries. On the river-bank below the city rose a monastery with an adjoining *stūpa*, both founded by the first wife of the Great Satrap Rājūla at the beginning of our era. Farther south stood another Buddhist convent which was conspicuous for the splendour of its sculptural ornamentation. Its founder was no less a personage than Huvishka, who held sway after Kanishka over the powerful realm of the Kushānas.

The hill at the west end of the present city is known by the name of Katrā, the 'Market'. This was the site of a third Buddhist sanctuary called Yaśa-vihāra. It must have been in existence as late as the sixth century. Subsequently, a Hindu temple sacred to Vishnu arose on the spot. This shrine, named Kesab Dev, was demolished in 1670 and replaced by a mosque. Near by stood, in the early days, a *stūpa* enclosed within a richly sculptured balustrade, of which a number of pillars have been recovered. These are the well-known railing pillars of Bhūtesar.

These buildings have been destroyed so ruthlessly that no data are left for the reconstruction even of their ground-plan; we can, however, form some idea of what they must have looked like with the help of reliefs on which similar edifices are represented. Thus we know the character of the Mathurā *stūpa*, miniature models of which have also been recovered. It differed from the *stūpa* of Central India by its more slender shape, but otherwise showed the same peculiarities. It was also enclosed within a stone balustrade, the construction of which resembled in detail the railings of Bharhut and Sānchi. The same is true of the gates or *toranas*. The decoration, too, of the balustrades and gates reveals a close relationship between the school of Mathurā and the older national art. The projecting ends of the cross-beams of the *toranas* are frequently adorned with figures of *makaras* (Plate 13*a*), though of a type somewhat different from those of Bharhut. The latter still retain the character of the crocodile, which at Mathurā has been almost entirely lost.

The ornamentation of the pillars—lotus-rosettes, palmettes, and fantastic animals—bears a strong resemblance to Bharhut motifs. But the Mathurā sculptors had a preference for female figures, which they represented in various graceful attitudes (Plate 12). This was not, indeed, an innovation. The origin of these pillar figures must, doubtless, be sought in the Yakshinīs who guard the gates of the sanctuary at Bharhut. Just as these do, they too often stand under a blossoming tree holding on to a branch with one uplifted hand. But there is a striking difference in character between the stately gate-keepers of Bharhut and the sensuous nymphs of Mathurā, whose carnality jars painfully with the austere spirit of Buddha's doctrine. The pillars of Bhūtesar are especially conspicuous by their luxuriant sculpture. No wonder that early archaeologists saw nautch girls in these female figures, although this interpretation could not easily be reconciled with their standing on the backs of misshapen dwarfs. Grünwedel, entirely because of their erotic character, refused to recognize them as Buddhistic. However, since *jātakas* are portrayed on the reverse side, a circumstance which was unknown to the German scholar, we are forced to assume that they actually formed part of a Buddhist monument.

A study of the railings, many parts of which have been recovered, is sufficient to prove that the Mathurā school must be considered as a direct development of the early sculpture of Central India. It is, therefore, fundamentally Indian. The art of Mathurā, nevertheless, contains several elements which point to Western influence. This is especially evident in a few sculptured groups, such as the Heracles with the Nemean lion, and the so-called Bacchanalian group, of which two examples have been found not far from the city of Mathurā. The former is a very feeble copy of a well-known Hellenistic motif, the latter a more felicitous representation of a corpulent Silenus with his satellites. Strange though it may seem, there is no doubt as to their provenance from a Buddhist sanctuary. The drunken Silenus probably figured as a prince of the Yakshas with his retinue.

These specimens, however, should not be considered as characteristic of the school of Mathurā. Too much attention, perhaps, has been paid to them by Western archaeologists. They do not justify the conclusion that Mathurā was more directly influenced by Hellenic art than was Gandhāra. On the contrary, it is clear that the foreign elements which we noticed reached Mathurā by way of Gandhāra, and that consequently the former received a second-hand, and consequently weakened, imprint.

Historical data enable us to account for this course of events. Family ties and a common faith formed a bond between the satraps of Taxila and Mathurā. It is probably not a mere accident that close by the monastery on the Jamnā, which was founded by the wife of a Great-Satrap, the drum of a small *stūpa* has been found which clearly betrays Gandhāran influence. It is adorned all around with eight scenes from the life of Buddha, which, in the manner of Graeco-Buddhist art, are separated by miniature pillars.

We may say in general that, wherever we meet with representations of the Buddha legend at Mathurā, they are apparently copies of compositions created by the sculptors of Gandhāra. This is also the case with the scenes of Buddha's Nativity and Nirvāna. The number of such reliefs, however, is extremely small as compared with the rich diversity that is found in Gandhāra. The treatment, moreover, is clumsy and lifeless. An important feature is the representation of the Buddha not by means of a symbol but in his own person, in the very centre of the composition. Here again Gandhāran influence is unmistakable.

Mathurā has produced numerous Buddha images of various dimensions. The question arises whether these, too, must be considered as imitations of Graeco-Buddhist statuary. This is certainly the case in one special category, portraying the Buddha wrapped in a monk's robe which reveals in its conventionalized drapery the influence of Western art. The pedestal of sitting figures is sometimes adorned with a relief representing a Bodhisattva seated in the attitude of meditation between devotees who bring him offerings. Here again Gandhāran influence is undeniable. A statuette of this kind found among the ruins of the Jetavana monastery, near Śrāvastī, must, by the testimony of the material, be the work of a Mathurā craftsman (Plate 11). We learn from the inscription that it was presented to the monastery by a citizen of Sāketa[2] called Sihadeva. From the evidence of the script it may be inferred that the statue dates from the third century of our era.

Besides these icons in the monk's folded robe there occurs another type in which the upper garment leaves the right shoulder and neck bare, while the drapery is scarcely indicated by a few parallel lines. The treatment of the hair is another distinctive feature of this type. The seated Buddha of the Katrā is a striking and well-preserved specimen (Plate 10). It may be dated from the beginning of the Kushāna period (first century of our era) on the strength of the characters used in the inscription on the pedestal. It is surprising that this inscription refers to the image as a Bodhisattva, although the foliage of the Bodhi tree clearly delineated around the nimbus would mark the figure a Buddha.

There are also standing images of this kind, such as the more than life-size statue that was excavated at Sārnāth in the year 1904. In the inscription it is stated that a monk named Bala, who must have been an inhabitant of Mathurā, erected it at Benares 'on

[1] Now Saheth-Maheth. [2] Another name for Ayodhyā.

the *chankrama*[1] of the Lord' in the third year of Kanishka's reign. This image, too, is called a Bodhisattva. It probably stood in the open air, protected by a stone parasol which has been recovered not far from the statue.

It is hardly conceivable that this local kind of Buddha, or, to quote the inscriptions, Bodhisattva, should have originated independently of the first-mentioned type. We should otherwise have to assume that the Buddha image had been created simultaneously at two different spots, in Gandhāra and at Mathurā. This, in itself, is highly improbable, but the two types, though differing in certain details, show such striking traits of resemblance that one cannot escape the conclusion that one must have evolved from the other.

Mathurā possesses yet another kind of images representing male beings adorned with rich head-gear and a profusion of ornaments. These are doubtless related to the princely figures of Gandhāra, and must, consequently, represent Bodhisattvas. Amongst them the future saviour Maitreya may be recognized by the ambrosia vase which he holds in his right hand, the same pose in which he appears in Gandhāra. In these images also dependence on Graeco-Buddhist art is unmistakable.

This dependence can also be noticed in the

[1] Place where according to tradition the Buddha had walked up and down in meditation.

decorative devices, some of which are strongly indianized imitations of motifs that Gandhāra had borrowed from Hellenistic art. Among these occur the Corinthian capital, the acanthus, the vine leaf, the merman, and the garland-bearers (Plate 13*b*). But there are other motifs that are genuinely Indian or that occur, at any rate, in the earliest national art of Central India, such as the stylized lotus, the palmette, the *aśoka* leaf, the railing, the vase of fortune and numerous other auspicious symbols, and various fantastic monsters such as the *makara*, *suparna*, and *vyālaka*, which were already in vogue in early Indian art.

The Mathurā school, like that of Gandhāra, exhibits a combination of foreign and native elements; but its fundamental character is essentially Indian, and evolved, as we saw, from the national sculpture of Central India. It lacks the naïve freshness of that older art, but excels it by greater skill in plastic portrayal. Western influence, which is so characteristic of Gandhāra art, is here only secondary, and the foreign elements are less conspicuous, since they have been largely absorbed as the result of a growing tendency towards indianization.

The Buddha image may have originated in Gandhāra but the sculptors of Mathurā, while copying it, transformed it into something quite different. We must not lose sight of the fact that for a couple of centuries sculptors had been at work at Mathurā.

The Yaksha images of that earlier period are marked by an archaic clumsiness and rigidity such as we also find in the earliest Buddha images. Another striking feature is that in both these categories the image is carved also on the back, which is never the case in the Graeco-Buddhist art of Gandhāra.

Although the aesthetic value of Mathurā sculpture during the rule of the Kushānas does not rate very high, its importance for the history of Buddhist art is beyond dispute. We saw that early in Kanishka's reign a Bodhisattva image was brought from Mathurā to the Deer Park at Benares. A similar image with a stone parasol was erected by the same donor, the monk Bala, in the Jetavana of Śrāvastī. In several other spots on the Gangetic plains fragments of sculpture have been recovered which are carved in the yellow-flecked red sandstone of Mathurā. Such pieces have also been found in Sānchi and as far north as Taxila. As late as the fifth century a colossal image of the dying Buddha was erected at Kusinārā[1] on the site of the Teacher's Nirvāna. The inscription states that it was the work of one Dinna, a sculptor of Mathurā. These few examples will suffice to show that Mathurā, in the first centuries of our era, was the great centre from which Buddhist art spread over the entire region of the Ganges and far beyond.

[1] Sanskrit: Kuśanagara. The site of Buddha's Nirvāna is near the village of Kasia in the Gorakhpur district, U.P.

V

The South-Indian Art of Amarāvatī
(A.D. 150–300)

IN the year 1797 there was discovered on the right bank of the Kistna, about sixty miles from its mouth, a Buddhist edifice that might be counted among the greater and most beautiful monuments of Indian Buddhism. It was then, probably, for the most part intact, for it had lain buried under the dust of the ages. But, unfortunately, a petty raja selected a neighbouring spot on the river for a new residence, and he found in the Buddhist shrine a welcome means of supplying himself, at small cost, with excellent building material. Not only was the entire *stūpa* razed to the ground but also the exquisitely sculptured pillars and panels were ruthlessly demolished and partly, it seems, even burnt to lime.

British archaeologists succeeded in rescuing part of the precious sculptures. Seven beautiful pieces reached the Indian Museum at Calcutta as early as 1797. Later on, 160 pieces were shipped to England; they now adorn the great staircase of the British Museum. Dr. Burgess examined the site of the old sanctuary in 1881 and collected 400 more, sadly damaged in part, which are now preserved in the museum at Madras.

The ancient building was so thoroughly levelled

with the ground that the excavators were not even able to reconstruct the original ground-plan with absolute certainty. The place where it had stood was merely indicated by a circular pit of about 75 yards in diameter. Rectangular projections pointed east, west, north, and south. Around the monument ran a procession path of fully 4 yards in width. It was originally enclosed within a richly sculptured balustrade nearly 4 yards high. The surface of the *stūpa*-drum all along the inner side of the ambulatory was also decorated with a series of rectangular bas-reliefs—a circumstance which misled the first investigators into believing that there had been two concentric railings.

These scanty data can be considerably supplemented with the aid of the sculptured fragments. The edifice was decorated with large rectangular panels on each of which the sculptor had portrayed a *stūpa* (Plate 14). One may safely assume that these very detailed effigies convey a faithful picture of the great monument that they were meant to decorate. They show a high, bell-shaped edifice surmounted by a square *harmika,* which supports two parasols. Most of its surface is covered with rows of bas-reliefs; the upper series apparently relates to the cycle of legends concerning the Buddha's Nativity.

It deserves notice that these relief belts, which encircle the *stūpa,* are interrupted, in the middle of the miniature dome, by a projection consisting of a large panel at the base and an oblong panel above it; the latter carries five pillars that somewhat resemble organ pipes.[1] A similar projection surmounted by a row of free standing columns is likewise indicated on both ends of the *stūpa*-dome. It is clear that we have here the explanation of the four rectangular projections noticed by Dr. Burgess in the ground-plan of the large *stūpa*. The miniature model, it is true, shows only three such projections, but the fourth one must, of course, be imagined in the centre of the invisible half of the dome.

The miniature *stūpa* in the relief is surrounded by a profusely decorated railing, which follows the contour of the central sanctuary and, accordingly, represents a balustrade of circular plan. Facing the four projections of the *stūpa* are the entrances to the procession path, which are formed by the balustrade bending outwards on either side. It is a remarkable fact that the south Indian *stūpa* knew nothing of the *toraṇa*. The square terrace of the northern *stūpas* is likewise absent and, consequently, also the flight of steps that leads up to it. Hence in its architectural peculiarities the *stūpa* of Amarāvatī has preserved a fairly primitive character.

The great balustrade, too, followed the original type in the main features of its construction. It consists of posts or pillars, about 3 yards in height, which

[1] In the inscriptions of Jaggayyapeta such pillars are called *āyaka-khambha*.

are connected by cross-bars and covered by a continuous coping. The decoration of this monument has been carried to an unparalleled extreme of richness and refinement.

On the outside both pillars and cross-bars are thickly covered with beautifully carved lotus-rosettes alternating with gambolling dwarfs in various attitudes. On the inside the ornamentation is even more varied. The central lotus-rosette of the pillars is here replaced by a medallion containing some story-telling relief, while the space above and beneath is occupied by smaller panels likewise representing either an episode from the Buddha legend or some *jātaka*. Along the inner side of the coping there runs a series of sculptured scenes, while outside it is decorated with the motif of the garland-bearers. This is of Hellenistic origin, but after its migration, by way of Gandhāra and Mathurā, to the banks of the Kistna, it is hardly recognizable in the fantastic shape it there evolved. The garland was transformed into a waving, strangely decorated scroll which is carried by dwarfish-looking men in Indian garb, who seem to be running at great speed. The spaces left vacant between the curves of the waving scroll are filled with various symbols such as a Bodhi tree, a Wheel of the Law, a *stūpa*, a five-headed Nāga, or a Garuḍa. It is a remarkable instance of complete indianization of a Western motif.

The illustrative reliefs are chiefly concerned with

the Buddha legend, which is here portrayed with great vividness and elaboration. One recognizes many a familiar episode in these panels which, unfortunately, have often come down to us in a sadly mutilated condition.

One excellently preserved piece, in the Indian Museum at Calcutta (Plate 15), represents three scenes from the beginning of the legend—the descent of the future Buddha. The first panel shows him as Bodhisattva enthroned in the Tushita heaven and surrounded by heavenly attendants who are rendering him homage. In the next we see him being carried through the sky in the shape of an elephant. He is supported by Yakshas in the midst of a swarming crowd of jubilant gods, who dance and make music. Next to this follows Queen Māyā who, asleep on her bed among a group of her female attendants, sees in her dream the Bodhisattva descend in the shape of a white elephant. This incident has also been portrayed by the sculptors of Bharhut and Gandhāra, in Bharhut with almost grotesque clumsiness, in Gandhāra with uninspired realism. But here are neither clumsiness nor lack of inspiration. The artists of Amarāvatī possessed imagination and plastic skill such as, even in India, have never been excelled.

Another splendid specimen of their art is a relief in the museum of Madras (Plate 17). It shows, in a circular frame, the Buddha's encounter with the mad elephant egged on by his wicked cousin Devadatta to destroy him. The centre of the scene is not occupied by the Buddha, but by a group of frightened citizens who are trying to escape from the dangerous beast. The Buddha is seen approaching from the right side. The elephant has been pictured twice, first in his rage seizing a man with his trunk, and again, devoutly kneeling before the Master. This duplication reminds one of the art of Sānchi, as does the love of irrelevant detail. But the pathos which the artist of Amarāvatī has expressed in this panel is lacking both in the old national art and in the jejune representations which the Graeco-Buddhist sculptors gave of such a dramatic incident from the Master's career.

A stele, which is also in the museum at Madras, presents the four principal events of Buddha's life (Plate 16*a*). Tradition, which had fixed the formula of these four scenes, did not allow full play to the artist's imagination. The limited space, moreover, forced him to conciseness. But in spite of these handicaps he achieved a certain measure of originality. The uncouth birth-scene is here replaced by the great departure from Kapilavastu,[1] which might be called the Buddha's spiritual birth. Next follows the Bodhi, in which Buddha is not menaced by Māra's host of demons but tempted by his seductive daughters. In the third scene, the sermon at Benares,

[1] It is interesting to compare this panel with those of Sānchi and Gandhāra (pp. 15, 21), in which the same subject has been treated but in quite a different manner.

the Master's audience consists, surprisingly, of persons in princely attire, instead of the five hermits of sacred tradition. In the fourth and topmost panel the Nirvāna is not represented by the dying Buddha, but by the *stūpa* in which his remains were interred and worshipped.

Another stele (Plate 16*b*), of which the upper half is lost, illustrates, in its remaining panels, the edifying legend of the conversion of Buddha's half-brother Nanda. This story has been told at great length in the *Saundarananda*, a famous Sanskrit poem[1] by Aśvaghosha, the great poet of Buddhism. The fame of this epic may perhaps account for the frequent treatment of the Nanda episode by the sculptors of Gandhāra and Amarāvatī. The story begins in the two half-panels at the foot of the stele. We first see young Nanda in the company of his beautiful bride, whom he assists at her toilet, and, in the next scene, reluctantly on his way to the monastery, carrying the begging bowl of his inexorable brother. The relief that follows evidently shows how he is ordained as a monk against his will.

The pieces discussed thus far reveal that in the art of Amarāvatī Buddha is represented in bodily form in the manner of the northern schools of Gandhāra and Mathurā. The earlier symbolic method, however, is also applied sometimes, as in the Nirvāna

[1] An English translation by Dr. E. H. Johnston was published by the Oxford University Press in 1932.

scene on the stele in Plate 16*a*. In this connexion it may be mentioned that, as appears from a few preserved fragments, Amarāvatī must have possessed a more ancient Buddhist monument which probably dated from the first or second century B.C.

The large *stūpa* which was discovered in 1797 and, unfortunately, promptly demolished, must have been erected in the latter half of the second century of our era. This is clear from the inscriptions, one of which is dated in the reign of King Pulumayi II (A.D. 138–70) of the Āndhra dynasty. The *Mahāchetiya*, as it is called in the inscriptions, must have been still in existence as late as the thirteenth century. An epigraphic document of that time refers to 'the lofty Chaitya beautifully adorned with a variety of sculpture'.

Other Buddhist ruins discovered along the lower Kistna testify to the ascendancy which the Good Law enjoyed in this region during the early centuries of our era.

Not far from the village of Jaggayyapeta, thirty miles to the north-west of Amarāvatī, there once stood a *stūpa* which had been founded by a certain Siddhattha during the reign of King Siri-Virapurisadatta of the Ikkhāku (Sanskrit Ikshvāku) dynasty. We know this from a Prākrit inscription incised on three stone columns which have been found on the spot. These columns, called *āyaka-khambha* in the inscriptions, must have occupied the same position on this monument as the four times five pillars which, according to the relief reproduced in Plate 14, once adorned the *stūpa* of Amarāvatī.

At some distance above Amarāvatī, on the right bank of the Kistna, lies a very important group of Buddhist ruins, which were excavated in the years 1927–30 by the English archaeologist Mr. A. H. Longhurst. This investigator discovered a large *stūpa* or *Mahāchetiya*, two temples (*chetiya-ghara*) of the old absidal type, three monasteries, and a few smaller monuments. The large *stūpa* shows the same ground-plan as that of Amarāvatī; it has four rectangular projections which must once have supported four sets of five *āyaka-khambhas*. These were, for the greater part, recovered on the four sides of the *stūpa* and appeared to contain extensive dedicatory inscriptions in Prākrit stating that the *Mahāchetiya* was founded by queens and princesses belonging to the Ikshvāku dynasty. The foundation probably took place in the third century of our era.

Mr. Longhurst also unearthed a number of richly sculptured architraves and steles which must have belonged to the smaller monuments. The sculptures consist of series of panels in which, either in horizontal or vertical order, the life of Buddha, several *jātakas*, and other edifying stories, partly unidentified, have been portrayed.

In Plate 18 we reproduce a relief of Nāgārjunikonda, depicting Buddha's first sermon in the Deer

Park at Benares. According to the old synoptic method, the two successive phases of the episode are represented in one panel. On the right we see the Buddha entering the park, reverently greeted by the five ascetics who were the first to be initiated into his doctrine. On the left he sits enthroned on a high seat and proclaims 'the Four Noble Truths' to the same five. One of them is shown to possess the supernatural faculties of an Arhat by ascending into the sky. In these two scenes the Buddha is accompanied by a satellite, in whom we recognize the Vajrapāni of Gandhāra.[1] The most striking feature of this panel is the original way in which a traditional subject has been treated.

Nāgārjunikonda represents a phase of Amarāvatī art which is, perhaps, less perfect and refined, but still full of life and inspiration.

Among these productions of genuine Indian art there occur a few figures which clearly reveal Western influence. This is, indeed, not surprising in an age when sea-borne trade connected the coasts of India with the Roman Empire. Moreover, one of the inscriptions of Nāgārjunikonda refers to a locality, Kantakasola, which must be identical with 'the emporium Kantakassula' mentioned by Ptolemy. Yet there is something queer in the appearance of a

[1] In the Graeco-Buddhist sculptures of Gandhāra Buddha is invariably accompanied by a savage-looking person carrying a *vajra* or thunder-bolt.

Scythian warrior with helmet and spear, or of a half-naked man with a drinking horn (*rhyton*) in his hand, among the sculptures which have come to light on this site and which are mostly permeated with the fragrance of Buddhist piety. The edifice, however, which these quaint sculptures once served to decorate, appears not to have borne a sacred character.

VI

The Golden Age during the Gupta Dynasty (A.D. 300—600)

A LARGE part of northern India remained for centuries under the sway of foreign dynasties, but in A.D. 320 there appeared in Bihār a royal house of native origin which gradually extended its power over the entire Aryan North. This was the imperial Gupta dynasty, whose scions bear names ending in *Gupta*. They were not Buddhists but adherents of Brahmanism, and their rule consequently coincided with a revival of the ancient Vedic worship and with the decline of Buddhism, which had flourished thanks to the patronage of powerful rulers such as Aśoka and Kanishka.

The reign of the Gupta dynasty was a period of literary and artistic efflorescence. Kālidāsa, the poet of the *Śakuntalā*, must have lived in this age. Through him the drama and lyrical poetry attained their acme. Sculptural art, at the same time, unfolded itself in unparalleled beauty and richness.

Buddhist art, too, must have benefited by this revival of artistic achievement. Although the Good Doctrine was now deprived of princely favour, its adherents, who belonged largely to the merchant class, must have shared in the general prosperity

[1] In reality the rule of the Gupta emperors lasted until the Hun invasions about the middle of the fifth century, but the Gupta style survived the fall of the Empire.

which Āryāvarta enjoyed under the strong, centralized administration of a native dynasty. The Gupta kings, though they were Brahmanists, were not hostile to Buddhism, nor is there any evidence of religious persecution. It was not until the second half of the fifth century, when India was ravaged by the invading Huns, that the great Buddhist monasteries were laid in ashes.

The high standard of Buddhist art in those days may be gauged by the Buddha image which then, entirely freed from the stigma of its alien origin, became the purest expression of absolute mental repose achieved by the subjugation of the flesh.

In Mathurā the somewhat coarse and clumsy image of the Kushāna period now develops into a thing of exquisite beauty. A good specimen is the life-size statue that the monk Yaśadinna dedicated in the fifth century (Plate 19). The delicate folds of the transparent garment are treated decoratively in Indian style. The original meaning of the nimbus was evidently no longer understood, for this disk of light is covered all over with concentric bands of graceful ornament in which festoons and foliage alternate with conventional flowers.

The profusely decorated halo is a special feature of the Buddha figure of the Gupta period. We notice it also in the images found at Sārnāth near Benares. A sublime example is the preaching Buddha (Plate 20), an exquisitely stylized figure, the drapery being suggested only by a delicate groove along the neck, wrists, and ankles. The background of this ethereal image is formed by the throne, which is adorned with *makara*-heads and standing lions. The nimbus is decorated with a broad band of floral and foliated ornament of rare beauty. The wheel symbol, placed between two couchant deer upon the pedestal in the midst of six worshippers, indicates that the seated figure is the Buddha Śākyamuni preaching his doctrine for the first time. For it was in the Deer Park at Benares that he 'set going the Wheel of the Law'.

In his account of the monastery of the Deer Park the Chinese pilgrim Hiuen Tsiang notes a life-size statue of copper showing the Buddha in the act of turning the Wheel of the Law which was enshrined in the principal temple. Metal images must indeed once have existed in large quantities in Buddhist India, but only very few specimens have survived. A copper statue of colossal size (height 7 feet 2½ inches) which represents Buddha standing in the attitude of imparting protection, came to light in 1862 in the chapel of a ruined monastery not far from Sultānganj on the lower Ganges. It is now preserved in the Art Museum of Birmingham. An inscribed seated Buddha statuette of brass inlaid with silver and copper, a work of the sixth century now in the Lahore Museum, is remarkable for its very elaborate pedestal wrought *à jour*.

The spot where Buddha preached his doctrine for the first time was of old one of the four great places of Buddhist pilgrimage. During fourteen centuries countless monuments were erected here, and their crumbling ruins still cover a widespread area. In the midst of this field of ruins still rises a massive relic-shrine, the Dhamēkh, which even in its decayed condition is able to create a deep impression. It rises to a height of 112 feet, and is to a large extent still faced with a mantle of red sandstone, which is decorated with broad bands of graceful and amazingly rich ornament. The style of this decoration makes it certain that this *stūpa* in its present form must be a monument of the Gupta period. The eight niches in the stone facing must once have contained as many images.

Very few of the sacred buildings have escaped destruction and neglect. But excavations at Sārnāth have revealed a profusion of sculpture, the larger part of which may be ascribed to the Gupta period. One gets the impression that the Buddha image, which in ancient times did not exist at all, acquired during this period an ever-increasing prominence in the Buddhist cult. The Teacher's image, distinguished by the various mystical hand-postures (*mudrās*), must have stood in the focus of religious worship, but by its side the Bodhisattvas, too, claimed the devotion of the faithful. In imitation of Gandhāra, the art of this period likes to place the Buddha between two of these divine saviours. Most popular among them were Maitreya and Avalokiteśvara.

The latter Bodhisattva is represented in an image of rare perfection, a masterpiece of Gupta art (Plate 21). In his headgear he carries the figurine of his spiritual father, the Buddha Amitābha. His left hand still holds the lotus-stalk, the flower of which has vanished. The right arm is also missing; but the open palm of the hand still makes the gesture of imparting bounty, by which Avalokiteśvara can be recognized. Beside the foliage of the lotus-flower which supports the Bodhisattva, the emaciated figures of two *pretas*[1] are shown kneeling with their hands folded in supplication, as if they were anxious to catch the nectar trickling down from the right hand of the Great Compassionate.

As the icons grow in number the scenes from the Buddha legend disappear almost completely from the sculptural art of this period. The *jātakas*, too, are very seldom illustrated. It would be rash, however, to jump at the conclusion that the life-story of the Teacher and the touching accounts of his previous existences had lost their charm. For it was in this very period that the walls of the caves of Ajānta were covered with frescoes in which both the former lives and the last existence of the Buddha Śākyamuni

[1] *Pretas* (Pali *peta*) are spirits of the dead who, in punishment of wicked deeds, are tormented by hunger and thirst in the life hereafter. See Wilhelm Stede, *Die Gespenstergeschichten des Peta Vatthu*, Leipzig, 1914.

were portrayed with painstaking care. The art of painting lent itself much better to the expression of the pathos of these edifying stories, and it was perhaps owing to the full development of that medium that the sculptors looked elsewhere for subject matter more gratifying to their skill.

During this period the illustrative relief, once the glory of Gandhāra and Amarāvatī, is almost entirely restricted to steles, on which the four principal moments of the Buddha legend are carved in vertical order, the Nirvāna, portrayed in the dying Buddha, crowning the whole (Plate 22).

These scenes, which had become stereotyped by agelong tradition, lack the vivid realism of the earlier art. Their character, however, is still primarily illustrative. Sometimes the sculptors felt the need of enriching the central event by the insertion of minor happenings. Thus the Nativity is enlivened by a scene of the new-born Buddha being sprinkled with water by two Nāgas. Here Indian art reverts to the primitive method of synoptic illustration, which it had reluctantly abandoned under Western influence.

One gets the impression that this kind of sculpture, which was probably executed by order, was not the artist's favourite work. He was especially attracted by purely decorative art, in which the Indian sculptor has ever excelled but which, in the age of the Guptas, reached a remarkable degree of excellence. We select a few pieces from the profusion which at one time must have made the sanctuaries of the Deer Park a delight to the eyes.

The preaching Buddha of Sārnāth, as we saw, sits in front of a frame whose upper bar is supported by two standing lions of heraldic shape. Such decorative animals, called *vyālaka*, are a common feature both of Buddhist and Brahmanical art. They were also introduced into Java where they form a frequent decorative motif in the reliefs of Barabudur. The excavations at Sārnāth have brought to light several detached specimens of *vyālaka* figures carved in relief. These pieces, too, were probably intended for the decoration of Buddha images. The two examples reproduced in Plate 23 will convey an idea of the imaginative power that inspired the artist of the Gupta period. The heraldic monsters have, in their graceful outline, retained their decorative effect but they have, at the same time, become living beings. In his search for ever greater wealth of decorative motifs the sculptor has given to each of his horned lions a brave swordsman for a rider, while another warrior seizes hold of the tail.

A fragment that probably formed part of the framework of a temple entrance displays the decorative art of the Gupta period in its full splendour (Plate 24). The many-sided shaft of the column, girded with beautifully ornamented bands, must have formed the post of the gateway. Adjoining it stands a vertical part of the frame adorned with amorous couples, each group being supported by a trio of corpulent dwarfs. A narrower frame, next to this, contains a series of small panels filled with similar fantastic creatures that are merrily dancing and making music, and the outer frame, which is of greater width, is adorned with a winding branch and graceful foliage encircling tiny human figures.

This exquisite piece of sculpture reveals not only a delicate sense for decorative art but also a sparkling joy of life little akin to the austere spirit of Buddhism. Yet the art of the Gupta age remains free from the oppressive sensuality that appears in some of the sculptures of Mathurā. With all its incredible wealth and diversity the decorative art of this period is marked by moderation and good taste and never degenerates into the surcharged ornamentation of later ages.

Gupta art may be compared with the poetic diction of Kālidāsa, who applies rhetorical ornament with much variety but always with the necessary restraint. In the poetry of later imitators, on the other hand, the story is choked by a rank growth of tasteless and insipid ornamentation. The decorative motif becomes predominant and the poetic story is reduced to a mere framework for its unrestrained indulgence. A similar process occurs in the architecture and sculpture of a later day, when the dominant lines of construction and composition are often buried under an overwhelming and bewildering profusion of ornament.

VII

The Buddhist Cave Temples
(50 B.C.—A.D. 700)

OUR sketch of Buddhist art in India would be incomplete without an account, however brief, of the sanctuaries that were hewn out of the living rock and which are commonly referred to as cave temples. This name is only partially correct. There are two kinds of Buddhist caves: *vihāras*, which served exclusively as residential quarters for the monks, and *chaitya*-halls (Sanskrit *chaitya-griha*, Pali *chetiya-ghara*), thus named because they enshrined, as an object of worship, a *chaitya* or *stūpa*, which was also cut out of the rock. Properly speaking, the name 'temple' is only applicable to the latter kind of caves. The *vihāras* or cave monasteries, however, partake of the character of temples in so far as they are usually provided with a chapel containing an image of the Buddha.

These *vihāras* and *chaitya*-halls show in their arrangement a close resemblance to the monasteries and temples constructed out of building materials. Of these, too, there must once have existed large numbers in India, but they have vanished with the religion that had created them. Now only a few ruins remain. Hence the cave monasteries and temples have special value as authentic and practically unchanged specimens of an almost lost architecture.

It is a point of special interest that the caves have preserved many traces of architecture in wood. In the earliest caves, which date back in part to the first century B.C., wood is found even where it could not have any constructive function in a rock-cut temple. There was no sense in lining the vaulted ceiling with wooden beams. In the later caves the original timber work was faithfully imitated in stone.

The earliest caves are marked by a noble simplicity and restraint in decoration. They belong to a period when the Buddha image had not yet been called into existence. If occasionally it does occur in these early caves, it is evidently a later addition. They form a distinct contrast to the later cave temples of the Gupta period, which are lavishly adorned with sculpture and assign a prominent place to the image of the Buddha.

One of the finest examples of the earliest period is the *chaitya*-hall of Kārli (first century B.C.), not far from Bombay (Plate 25). This cave temple is 44 yards deep and 15 feet in width. Its division into a spacious nave and two side aisles gives it a striking resemblance to a basilica. The place for the altar in the apse is occupied by a *chaitya* of simple shape surmounted by a wooden parasol. The central nave is separated from the side aisles by a double row of fifteen columns with vase-shaped bases and grooved bell-shaped capitals, which are decorated with elephants each carrying, in pairs, a man and a woman.

Another important group of early cave temples is found at Nāsik, the well-known place of pilgrimage on the upper Godāvarī. The Hindu population has connected these caves with the five Pāndavas, the heroes of the Mahābhārata. But there cannot be the slightest doubt as to their connexion with Buddhism. The two large *vihāras*, one of which bears a dedicatory inscription of Ushavadāta, the son-in-law of the satrap Nahapāna, have each a representation of a *stūpa* carved in relief on the back wall facing the entrance. One of the smaller *vihāras* is provided with a chapel, in which a Buddha sits enthroned between two Bodhisattvas. But it is clear from the style of the columns and pilasters that this chapel is a later addition of the Gupta period.

The façade of the *chaitya*-hall (Plate 26) is dominated by the large horseshoe window, through which the light is admitted. The decoration of this façade consists almost exclusively of architectural motifs—rows of *stūpas* alternating with pilasters, above these a repetition of the horseshoe arch, and finally the well-known motif of the railing, which was often decoratively applied in ancient Buddhist art.

The best-known groups of Buddhist caves are those of Ajānta and Ellora, both situated in the State of Hyderābād. At Ajānta there are no less than twenty-six, which are exclusively Buddhist but dating from various periods. The seven caves which form the centre of the entire group are of the primitive type we have just described. The others, which adjoin the original central group on either side, display a wealth of ornament in sharp contrast to the simplicity of previous days. They are not only profusely decorated with sculpture but the walls, columns, and ceilings were once covered also with painting, of which a large part has been preserved. It is especially on account of these frescoes that the name Ajānta has become famous in the history of Indian art. But the sculpture, too, which for the larger part belongs to the Gupta period, contributes in no small measure to the fame of these cave temples.

Especially beautiful is the decoration of the first two caves, which belong to the class of the *vihāras*. Through a richly adorned portico one enters a square hall lined on three sides by rows of cells, which once were inhabited by the monks. The cell facing the entrance is of a larger size than the others, for it must serve as an abode for the Buddha, whose image is enthroned here in the dark as preacher of the Good Law. The entrance to this *gandhakutī*[1] is guarded by two painted Bodhisattvas, one of which represents Avalokiteśvara and the other Vajrapāni.

The best-preserved mural paintings are found in two other *vihāra* caves (nos. 16 and 17 of the entire group). In one of these the entire wall on

[1] Gandhakutī, originally the name of Buddha's abode in the monastery Jetavana at Śrāvastī, became, later on, a term for a chapel or temple in which his image was placed.

the right side of the hall was once decorated with scenes of the Buddha legend, from the Conception to the Enlightenment, but these frescoes have now almost completely faded away. On the opposite wall has been portrayed the edifying story of Nanda's conversion. The so-called 'Dying Princess' is actually Nanda's bride, who bewails the separation from her husband.[1]

In the adjoining *vihāra* cave the frescoes, which decorate the four walls of the great hall, have been much better preserved. They are all illustrations of *jātakas*. The left wall presents in a series of scenes the touching story of Prince Viśvantara, the hero of bounteousness. The wall on the right bears a splendid illustration of the tale (*avadāna*) of Prince Siṃhala, the mythical ancestor of the Sinhalese of Ceylon.

In the portico of the last-mentioned *vihāra* cave a remarkable representation of the Wheel of Existence has been preserved in part. In the monasteries of the *lamas* in Tibet this is still a never-failing symbol which always occupies that very place.

There is a close connexion between the two monastic caves just described and the *chaitya*-temple (no. 19) which almost immediately adjoins them. A comparison of the façade of this sanctuary (Plate 27) with the front of the *chaitya*-cave of Nāsik (Plate 26) reveals a striking contrast between earlier simplicity and later exuberance. Another

[1] Cf. above, p. 44.

characteristic feature of this Ajānta art is the profusion of Buddha images. The faithful never tired of representing him, either standing or seated, with the various mystic hand-postures or *mudrās* prescribed by tradition. The large window, that has retained the horseshoe shape, is flanked by two corpulent figures. These are Yakshas who, as givers of wealth and prosperity, have always been entitled to worship by the people of India. Here they have even received a place beside the Buddhas.

No less popular were the Nāgas or snake demons who, as water-sprites and bringers of rain, had special importance for the tillers of the soil. They are usually portrayed as hybrid creatures, partly human, partly reptile; but Buddhist art both in India and Java represents them, as a rule, in human shape with a hood of snake-heads, which encircles the head like an aureole. Such a Nāga king accompanied by two female attendants is seen in a chapel to the left of the portico of the *chaitya*-hall described above, where, through the ages, he has received the floral offerings of the faithful (Plate 28).

A less-known group of Buddhist caves, apparently likewise dating from the Gupta period, is found near the village of Bāgh, forty miles west of Dhār in Mālwā. These are exclusively monastic caves, among which are a few of imposing dimensions. They have been hewn out of the rocky slope of a hill-side which rises on the north from the valley of the Narbadā;

but owing to the brittleness of the stone these rock dwellings have partly collapsed, to the detriment of the sculpture they contained. Here also the walls were once adorned with mural paintings which, to judge from the few fragments extant, must have been of great beauty. The most important one is found in the portico of one of the larger monastery caves. It represents a series of scenes from some unidentified story. The little that has been preserved, including a stately procession of horsemen and elephant-riders, bears a striking resemblance in style to the later frescoes of Ajānta and cannot differ much from these in age.

The most famous cave temples are those of Ellora, about ten miles to the north-west of Daulatābād. They cover an area which extends from north to south over a mile and a quarter. Three different religions are represented here: the southern group comprising fourteen caves is Buddhist, the middle one belongs to Brahmanism, the northernmost to Jainism.

The Buddhist group contains only one real temple, a large *chaitya*-hall, which is now known by the name of the Cave of Viśvakarma, the architect of the gods. It is a large *chaitya*-temple of the same type as the two halls of Ajānta (nos. 19 and 26). In certain respects it represents a more highly developed stage, which may justify us in assigning it to a somewhat later date (*c.* A.D. 700). It is interesting to notice that even in this late example the tradition of the ancient wood construction still lingers. The entire façade actually looks as if it had been built out of timber.

The southernmost and probably oldest group of small *vihāras* (nos. 2–4), which belong to the fourth or fifth century, is popularly known by the name of Dherawāra, in contradistinction to the large monastery cave which is called Mahāwāra. Two of the *vihāra* caves, the so-called Don Tal and Tin Tal, have three storeys. Tin Tal excels in richness of ornamentation.

Finally, mention should be made of the caves of Aurangābād, which represent the final phase in the long development through which this peculiar form of Buddhist art has passed. With the exception of one dilapidated *chaitya*-temple of a primitive type, these little-known monastery caves seem to belong to the same period as the latest caves of Ajānta (7th century A.D.). A striking feature of these later caves is the increasing prominence of the Bodhisattvas, who take their place beside the numberless Buddha images, especially Avalokiteśvara as Rescuer from 'the Eight Fears'. At Ellora and Aurangābād one also finds many figures of female Bodhisattvas, which do not yet occur at Ajānta.

VIII

Aftermath and Decline
(A.D. 600—1200)

WHEN the Gupta dynasty came into power the history of Indian Buddhism reached a turning-point. The old Vedic religion of the Brahmans, so closely connected with the entire organization of Indo-Aryan society, was revived and grew in prestige under the powerful protection of a native royal family. New temples and images dedicated to the gods of the Brahmanic pantheon bear witness to that revival.

The doctrine of Buddha, on the other hand, had spread, indeed, far beyond the confines of India and penetrated even into the countries of the Far East. But its very character as a cosmopolitan religion impaired its national vitality. Buddhism declined in India until, finally, about the year 1200, it succumbed before the inroads of triumphant Islām.

We need not expatiate on the various causes that combined in bringing about the downfall of Indian Buddhism. One of them was, no doubt, the loosening of the rigid monastic discipline, which in the early days had been prescribed to the minutest detail in rules attributed to the Buddha himself. In the plastic art of the Kushāna period one notices already a propensity to luxuriance which is little in keeping with the austere self-restraint of Buddha's doctrine.

The appearance of the Buddha image, an event of

prime importance in the development of plastic art, initiated at the same time a profound change in Buddhist worship. The ancient adoration of Buddha's relics was now supplemented by a new iconolatry which approximated Buddhism to Brahmanism. As early as the days of Aśoka a multiplicity of Buddhas had evolved from the historic Buddha, uniform divinities who differed only in name and who claimed their share in the homage of the faithful. Among these it was especially Maitreya, the successor of Śākyamuni, who occupied an independent place in the cult. The Chinese pilgrim Fā-hien saw, about A.D. 400, a gigantic image of Maitreya some 120 feet high in the northern border region of India.

Maitreya, the future Buddha, who is believed to dwell in the Tushita heaven, became the prototype of a host of similar celestial beings, spiritual sons of the Buddhas, who as saviours in distress inspired the ardent devotion of the pious. As early as the days of Fā-hien, the Chinese pilgrim just mentioned, this cult of the Bodhisattvas was in vogue.[1]

Not long afterwards female Bodhisattvas also appeared on the scene, among them the highly venerated goddess Tārā. Her numerous images bear evidence to the high esteem that she enjoyed in northern India. As early as the eighth century her cult had penetrated into the Indian Archipelago. The

[1] The pilgrim says, 'Adherents of the Mahāyāna sacrifice to Prajnāpāramitā, Manjuśrī, and Avalokiteśvara'.

oldest Buddhist inscription of Java, dated in the Śaka year 700 (= A.D. 778), refers to the foundation of a temple sacred to Tārā. It is the Chandi Kalasan, one of the masterpieces of Hindu-Javanese architecture.

The goddess Tārā, whose name implies her character of divine saviour, is a benign figure. She is usually portrayed in purely human shape, holding a lotus-flower in her left hand, whilst her right hand with open palm is held out in the gift-bestowing attitude. Some of her images belong to the very best that Buddhist art has produced during this period. Apart from her femininity, which is in itself a blemish according to ancient Buddhist conceptions, her character fits admirably into the cadre of Buddhist ethics.

But by the side of Tārā appear other female deities far less attractive in character and appearance, such as Mārīchī, also called Vajravarāhī or the She-Boar of the Thunder-bolt, who is portrayed with three faces (one being a swine's snout) and eight arms brandishing various weapons (Plate 30).

Generally speaking the iconography of this period shows an increasing tendency to represent Bodhisattvas and other divine beings with many heads and arms. The monstrous shape of the eleven-headed Avalokiteśvara, which has become so popular in Tibet, originated in India. It is found in one of the caves of Kanheri.

It is easy to see how Buddhism, by this development of polytheism and iconolatry, came ever closer to the popular form of Brahmanism. Various lower demons, which had probably haunted the consciousness of the masses for ages, were now admitted to the assembly of the gods and were given a definite shape in accordance with their frightful and repulsive character.

In spite of the decline that marks Buddhism from the Gupta period onwards, it would be incorrect to call the last six centuries of Indian Buddhism a period of artistic sterility. During the two hundred years which immediately followed the Gupta period (A.D. 600–800) Buddhist art had an aftermath in which the great traditions continued to be an inspiration.

It was especially at the principal places of pilgrimage that the religious life flourished, thanks to the steady flow of pilgrims from all over India and, in fact, from the whole Buddhist world. Until the very last temples and monastic buildings were founded in the Deer Park at Benares and in other sacred spots, often by persons of royal blood. Large *stūpas*, it seems, were no longer erected; but it was still considered a meritorious work to restore dilapidated *stūpas*, according to ancient custom, by means of a new mantle of stone.

Indian Buddhism retained its foothold longest in Magadha (now southern Bihār), where it had first taken rise. There were so many places here that had been sanctified by the presence of the Master. The holy fig-tree of Bodh Gayā was the focal point of the entire Buddhist world and the goal of thousands of pilgrims. Here stood the great temple of the Mahābodhi, surrounded by a multitude of minor monuments erected by pilgrims from various lands (Plate 33).

In Magadha, moreover, Buddhism enjoyed the royal protection of the Pāla dynasty, which ruled over this region from the eighth till the eleventh century. Next to Bodh Gayā, Nālandā was of the greatest importance to the Buddhism of this period. The Chinese pilgrim Hiuen-Tsiang praises, in the seventh century, the splendid architecture of the large monastery of Nālandā and the learning of the Buddhist monks who were its reṣidents. Systematic excavations in recent years have brought to light the ruins of these long-abandoned monastic buildings.

Indo-Buddhist art, too, found in Magadha a last refuge. It concentrated its activities primarily upon the great places of pilgrimage, where the pilgrims' demand for devotional offerings kept artistic production alive. It is especially icons that were produced in the last centuries of Buddhist worship in India. Buddha images were still the most numerous, but mass production tended to rob them of all spirituality. In the centuries that immediately followed the Gupta period Buddhism still produced, indeed, works of great merit such as the statuette from Kurkihār, now in the museum at Lucknow (Plate 29). It represents the Buddha seated under the Bodhi tree, whose foliage is visible around the oval aureole. The 'earth-touching' gesture of the right hand also indicates the moment of the Enlightenment. The strictly conventionalized figure is marked by simplicity and severity of line. The background, on the contrary, displays a profusion of decorative detail. The two standing leogryphs (*vyālaka*), which support the upper ledge of the back, have been placed on the top of small elephants, and above appear two mythological creatures, half man, half bird, known by the name of *kinnara*. This fine image, according to the inscribed dedication, was the gift of a resident of Benares called Vinītabuddhi, who probably lived in the ninth century.

While the Buddha images grew in number and were placed along the walls of the monuments with monotonous and meaningless repetition, presentments of the Buddha legend, which had been such an inexhaustible source of inspiration to the artists of former ages, became more and more scarce. Sometimes one finds the back-slab of the Buddha image decorated with representations of the four principal moments that formed such popular motifs in previous periods. But these episodes—birth, spiritual awakening, first preaching, and death—have shrunk to mere formulae devoid of illustrative vitality. Usually the image portrays the Buddha at a crucial moment of his life; but this is merely indicated by the gesture of the hand, or sometimes by some symbolic sign, while the figure itself remains unchanged in rigid immobility. When the outstretched right hand points down to the earth it indicates the moment before the Bodhi, when Buddha, challenged by Māra, called the earth goddess to witness. This great moment may be indicated still more definitely by the foliage of the Bodhi tree above the nimbus. Sometimes, also, Māra's demons are portrayed on either side of the Buddha, but reduced to such diminutive size that they have entirely lost their terrifying aspect.

When rendering the first preaching at Benares the sculptor expressed it by the *mudrā* of the Wheel of the Law and by the sign of the wheel between the two gazelles. When the Buddha is represented in a standing attitude between two little figures of the Hindu gods, Brahmā and Indra, we are reminded by these two satellites of the Buddha's descent from the heaven of the thirty-three gods where he had taught the Good Doctrine to his mother.

When we find him accompanied by the little figure of an elephant the reference is to the miracle of Rājagriha. But one would hardly recognize the raging Nālāgiri of the legend in the tiny elephant that kneels at the Buddha's feet. It is a far cry from the vivid portrayal of this episode in the art of Amarāvati[1] to this bare indication of the scene. It can hardly be dignified with the name of illustration. The little elephant, the host of demons, the wheel

[1] Cf. above, pp. 42 f.

with the gazelles, are merely symbols indicating the episodes which the sculptor had in mind. It is, indeed, worthy of note that Buddhist art, in its final stage, reverted to representation by means of symbols, a practice which characterized its earliest phase. But whereas in its beginning this symbolism was an expression of naïve, reverential awe, it proceeded in these final days of Indian Buddhism from lack of creative skill and barrenness of imagination.

Miniature painting of this period shows analogous symptoms of decline. Our knowledge of its pictorial art is limited to a few illuminated manuscripts from Nepāl, in which famous sanctuaries of the Buddhist world are indicated by pictures of the various divinities that were worshipped in those places. The principal episodes from the Buddha legend are treated in the same summary fashion that had become the vogue in sculptural art.[1]

The sculpture of this period achieves, indeed, considerable variety in the portrayal of the countless deities of diverse rank that figure in the immense Buddhist pantheon. But this variety is only external. The attitude, the number of arms and heads, the choice of emblems, have all become stereotyped according to rules which the sculptor had to follow minutely if the image made to order was not to fail of its beneficent effect. Genuine artistic inspiration had little part in the production of these images.

[1] A. Foucher, *Iconographie bouddhique* (1900), pp. 155 ff.

Images wrought in metal were also produced. We have quoted above two examples of the Gupta period, one a copper Buddha figure of more than natural size. Large-sized metal images were particularly liable to destruction during the age of Moslem supremacy, so that hardly any have survived. Of late years, however, large numbers of bronze figures of small size have come to light in the course of excavations at Nālandā. Collections of such statuettes have also been discovered at Kurkihār in southern Bihār and at Negapatam on the coast of Coromandel.

Small-sized stone *stūpas*, too, were made in large quantities at Bodh Gayā for the use, no doubt, of pious pilgrims. Such ex-votos are often decorated with rows of seated Buddhas for the purpose, perhaps, of enhancing the offering's magic effect. But sometimes one finds little monuments that reveal the sculptor's taste and artistic skill, such as a slender stone *stūpa* in the temple-court of Bodh Gayā (Plate 31). This is a fair specimen of the graceful type that in the final phase of Buddhist art developed from the ancient dome-shaped *stūpa* of Central India. The octagonal drum is supported by a subtly chiselled square basement with recessed corners, while the smooth cap-stone still retains somewhat the original shape of the Sānchi *stūpa*. In the cone-shaped ornament that crowns the whole one recognizes an accumulation of fourteen parasols which have been combined into one pinnacle. Each of the four broader faces of the octagonal drum contains a richly decorated niche, in which a crowned Buddha with crossed legs sits enthroned upon a lotus-seat. It is surprising that the great monk is here adorned with a diadem, jewelled ear-pendants, and necklaces.[1]

The same peculiarity appears in a fine piece of sculpture now preserved in the Ethnographic Museum at Munich (Plate 32). It has evidently formed part of a little monument such as we have just described. The Buddha is represented here at the crucial moment that immediately preceded the Bodhi, as is clearly indicated by his gesture and by the foliage of the sacred fig-tree which forms, as it were, a canopy above his head. Moreover, Māra's host is represented by the tiny demonic figures on either side of the immobile Buddha. Under the lotus-seat appears Māra himself with his bow and *makara*, and in the centre the earth goddess holding a vase in her hand.

On the spot of Buddha's Enlightenment there must, since early days, have stood a sanctuary. But the temple of the Mahābodhi (Plate 33) underwent, no doubt, profound changes in the course of repeated restoration. However that may be, this spot is still the centre of the Buddhist world and the goal of pilgrims from all countries where Buddhism yet prevails at the present day.

[1] Cf. Paul Mus, 'Le Buddha paré', *Bulletin de l'Ecole Française d'Extrême-Orient*, vol. xxviii, and L. Scherman, 'Buddha im Fürstenschmuck', *Abhandlungen der Bayerischen Akademie der Wissenschaften*, Phil.-hist. Abt., N. F. vii (1932), p. 21, Abb. 2.

IX

The Buddhist Art of Ceylon

ALTHOUGH Buddhism vanished from India about A.D. 1200, it has remained in a very ancient form the prevalent religion of Ceylon up to the present day. In consequence the early Buddhist monuments, which on the Indian continent too often fell a prey to cupidity and vandalism, have been preserved here and still command the veneration of the faithful as sacred shrines of the national religion. It is due to the disastrous effect of the incessant wars waged by the Sinhalese against the Tamil invaders that many a monument has come down to us in a sadly mutilated condition. It is true that in several instances the ruined *stūpas* and temples have been restored, but unfortunately the glaring aspect of the completely renovated sanctuaries is often far more painful than was their previous appearance of picturesque decay and venerable age. It is greatly to be deplored that in the difficult problem of preservation and restoration religious zeal has not always been guided by good taste. The archaeologist, moreover, has special reason to regret the wholesale renovations which are apt to efface completely the architectural features of the original building.

The study of the ancient Buddhist monuments of Ceylon receives valuable support from the two Pali chronicles *Dīpavaṃsa* and *Mahāvaṃsa* which, as they were composed by monks, give special attention to the *historia sacra* of the island and to the sacred foundations due to the piety of the Buddhist rulers of Lankā.[1]

These chronicles give an account of the introduction of Buddhism into Ceylon which, although interwoven with miracle and legend, may be accepted as fundamentally historical. It was owing to the religious zeal of the great Aśoka that the Good Law was brought to the island. There is all the more reason to accept this tradition as Aśoka in one of his rock-edicts mentions Tambapanni among the countries to which he had sent his emissaries for the propagation of Dhamma.

It was the Emperor's own son Mahinda who, according to the Pali chronicles, became the apostle of Ceylon. Accompanied by four other *arahats*, he transported himself through the air and alighted on the top of the Mount Mihintale, situated at a distance of eight miles to the east of the ancient capital Anurādhapura. In those days Devānampiya Tissa was the ruler of Lankā. He met the apostle of Buddhism on the summit of the rock and soon became his first convert.

It is on the sacred mountain of Mihintale, so closely associated with the advent of Buddhism in Ceylon, that some of the earliest monuments of that

[1] The name by which Ceylon is indicated in the chronicles.

religion are found. The Ambasthala Dāgaba, a *stūpa* of moderate size, is believed to contain the bones of Mahinda. An even more precious relic, a hair from the *ūrnā* of the Buddha himself, is enshrined in the Mahasāya, a structure of the same class but of much more imposing dimensions. These two early sanctuaries are of great religious interest but are of little value for the history of Buddhist architecture. The Ambasthala has been thoroughly renovated, whereas the restoration of the Mahasāya, begun some years ago, has made but little progress.

The two great centres of Buddhist art in Ceylon are Anurādhapura and Polonnaruwa, which succeeded each other as capitals of the Sinhalese kings of Lankā. The former town, situated in the centre of the northern half of the island, was the capital during the earlier period; it appears, however, that many of the ancient remains found here belong to a comparatively late date A.D. 800–1000.[1] The later medieval period centres mainly in Polonnaruwa, situated some fifty miles to the south-east of the earlier capital in the valley of the Mahaweli Ganga.

It is Anurādhapura which boasts the architectural and sculptural monuments not only earliest in date but also most impressive by their size and beauty. The *stūpas* by which the royal city was surrounded are

[1] It was not until *c.* A.D. 1000 that Anurādhapura was finally deserted. Cf. S. Paranavitana, 'The Capital of Ceylon during the ninth and tenth centuries' (*Ceylon Journal of Science*, Section G, vol. ii, pp. 141 ff.).

conspicuous on account of their gigantic dimensions. These enormous structures of solid brickwork testify to an incredible expense of patient labour, but do not rank high among the world's monuments of architectural art. In more than one instance they have been completely renewed by the addition of a fresh brick facing according to the practice followed throughout the history of Buddhist architecture.

Earliest among the sanctuaries of Anurādhapura is the Thūpārāma Dāgaba which is believed to have been built by Devānampiya Tissa himself as a receptacle of the Buddha's right collar-bone. On account of this holy relic it enjoys a special fame of sanctity. It is a small-sized *stūpa* which has been wholly renewed so that it is impossible to decide on its original aspect. It is surrounded by a cluster of stone pillars with exquisitely carved capitals which must once have carried a wooden superstructure.

Somewhat later in date is the famous Ruanwäli Dāgaba built by Dutthagāmani who must have reigned about 100 B.C. The *Mahāvaṃsa* devotes several chapters to a description of the building operations on the 'Mahāthūpa'—the 'Great Stūpa'—as it is called in the chronicle. From this account it may be inferred that the surface of the enormous solid dome of brickwork was originally profusely decorated with painting applied on a layer of white plaster. This decoration has entirely disappeared.[1]

[1] Two decorative motifs are mentioned in *Mahāvaṃsa*, xxxii. 4.

We may assume that the monument, although recently completely restored, still retains its chief architectural characteristics. The enormous dome measures 270 feet in height and as many feet in diameter at its base. Round the base of the bell there are three circular terraces *c.* 7 feet wide, and the whole pile is raised on a square platform 500 feet each way, which is decorated with some 400 elephant figures modelled in terra-cotta.[1]

The Mirisavätiya Dāgaba to the north of the Tissa Wäwa is also attributed to Dutthagāmani who built it after having slain Elāra, the Tamil invader, in single combat. Though smaller in size than the Ruanwäli it is a pile of imposing dimensions. In 1888–91 it was partly restored at the expense of a Siamese prince but is again falling into disrepair.

The largest building of this kind is the Jetavanārāma or Eastern Dāgaba which was built by the heretical king Mahāsena (A.D. 325–52) and completed during the reign of his son and successor Meghavanna. It stands on a square paved platform measuring some 600 feet both ways; the base is said to cover about 8 acres.

A fourth giant is the Abhayagiri or Northern Dāgaba which was built by King Vattagāmani Abhaya about 29 B.C. after his restoration to power.[2] It has

[1] Mr. Hocart has found definite evidence, especially at the Mirisavätiya Dāgaba, that the old type was circular and that the square platform is comparatively late.

[2] Mr. Ayrton has definitely proved that in the popular nomen-

still a height of 250 feet and measures 360 feet in diameter.

These four great monuments of Anurādhapura have retained a very early type of the Indian *stūpa*. They are hemispherical structures raised on a triple circular terrace. The superstructure, which in most cases has disappeared, was a cube carrying a tapering pinnacle likewise of brick masonry. The grooved pinnacle, which is connected with the cube by means of a narrow neck, still recalls the *harmika* with its row of stone parasols peculiar to the early *stūpas* of the Indian continent.

In one important point these *stūpas* of Ceylon differ from their prototypes of Central India. They are provided with four rectangular structures of considerable size projecting from the drum of the dome and facing the cardinal points. These projections are variously designated as altars, chapels, frontispieces, or screens,[1] but from this variety of terms it is evident that their purport is far from certain (Plate 34). It has been conjectured that they served as 'a screen to the steps leading upwards to the procession paths round the dāgaba'; but there does not seem to be any evidence that either steps or procession paths some distance up the dome actually did exist.

It has been noted above that the *mahāchetiyas* of

clature the names of the Abhayagiri and Jetavanārāma Dāgabas have been interchanged. Vide *Memoirs of the Archaeological Survey of Ceylon*, vol. i, p. 45.

[1] The Sinhalese term by which they are indicated is *vāhalkaḍa*.

Amarāvatī and Nāgārjunikonda consist of a solid dome and drum with four rectangular projections each of which must have carried five pillars which in the inscriptions are indicated by the technical name of *āyaka-khambha.* We may perhaps assume that the so-called 'altars, chapels, or screens' of the Ceylonese dāgabas had a similar purpose and that the *stūpa* type of Anurādhapura at any rate was derived from that of the Kistna valley. An inscribed stone found in the pavement at the southern 'altar' of the Northern Dāgaba records the construction of four *ayikas* by order of King Malu Tisa. There is good reason to assume that the term *ayika* refers to the rectangular projections in question.[1]

The so-called 'altars' of the Sinhalese *stūpas* have attracted attention on account of their sculptural decoration. They are universally faced with stone and show a number of superposed cornices sometimes supported by a series of ornamental brackets or by a row of elephant heads. Occasionally we find a frieze of running animals carved in low relief.

On both ends of the so-called 'altar' we find a high stele which in the case of the Mirisavätiya Dāgaba is surmounted by a seated lion figure carved in the round. The front of the stele is carved with a high stalk rising from a bulbous vase, perhaps a

[1] *Epigraphia Zeylanica*, vol. i, p. 252 and *Ceylon Journal of Science*, Section G, vol. ii, p. 4. Malu Tisa, called Kanittha-Tissa in the *Mahāvaṃsa*, reigned about A.D. 230.

mangalakalaśa, and provided with leaves alternating with human and animal figures set in pairs.

A stately Nāga figure is found on the side face of the stele at the Abhayagiriya Dāgaba.[1] It is noteworthy that side by side with the human Nāga, recognizable only from the hood of cobra heads, we find the polycephalous serpent in theriomorphic shape. A very fine example of the latter type is found at the same dāgaba. Evidently both types of Nāga figures have been derived from the Buddhist art of the Indian continent.

This is the case with other decorative devices of Sinhalese art such as the *makaras* employed in *makara-toranas* and in balustrades.

It is a point of special interest that the great Buddhist *stūpas* of Ceylon possess neither the railings[2] nor the *toranas* which are such conspicuous adjuncts of similar monuments in Central India, Mathurā, and Amarāvati. By their omission a great opportunity for sculptural decoration was lost. It is exclusively the

[1] Cf. H. W. Cave, *The Ruined Cities of Ceylon*, pp. 70–2.

[2] Fragments of a stone railing have come to light on the site of the Jetavanārāma Dāgaba. In its general construction it closely agrees with the Buddhist railings of India; but the posts, 7 ft. 6 in. high, are square and it has no decorative sculpture of any kind. The whole monument is rectangular in plan. Cf. Cave, op. cit., p. 82. Mr. Hocart has drawn attention to the probability of wooden railings having once been employed in Ceylon. There is one *stūpa* surrounded by a stone railing at Mādirigiriya in the North-Central Province. This railing is devoid of sculptural decoration.

so-called altar or screen which presented scope for the decorative skill of the sculptor.

There are, however, other monuments at Anurādhapura which have preserved exquisite specimens of sculptural art. In particular the flights of stone steps marking the entrance to most of the sacred buildings are works of rare beauty. Most conspicuous is the so-called moon-stone which is a semicircular slab forming the door-step and decorated with a procession of animals in which we recognize the same set of four—elephant, bull, lion, and horse—as are found on the abacus of the Aśoka capital of Sārnāth.[1] The best-preserved specimens belong to the so-called pavilion of Mahāsena's palace.[2]

The entrance is flanked by two guardstones carved with Nāga figures of a more elaborate and later type than those which decorate the 'screens' of the Abhayagiri Dāgaba. Whereas the latter have a hood consisting of five cobra heads, the Nāgas on the guardstones are distinguished by a nine- or elevenfold hood. Each of them lifts a vase on the palm of one hand, whilst the other hand grasps a lotus-stalk with a conventional flower.

Sculptures illustrating the Buddha legend or the *jātakas* appear to be almost unknown in Ceylonese art.[3] At the cave temple of Isurumuniya near the

[1] Cf. above, p. 11.

[2] Cave, op. cit., pl. XXIV.

[3] There is only one possible case of a *jātaka* on a balustrade at Anurādhapura. Two sculptures in the Amarāvatī style, now

embankment of the Tissa Wäwa (the artificial lake ascribed to Devānampiya Tissa) there are two curious reliefs (Plate 35). The one, cut out of the living rock and distinguished by a simple and severe style reminiscent of Pallava art, shows a male figure seated with his outstretched right arm resting on his knee. The head of a horse is visible over his shoulder.[1] The other, carved on a slab, represents an amatory couple, the female figure being rendered with great charm. Her male companion appears to be a warrior, from the sword and shield partly visible behind him. It is impossible to decide what subject these two reliefs represent; they do not betray any relation to Buddhist lore.

In the course of excavations at the Ruanwäli Dāgaba three standing Buddha images of more than life-size have come to light. The arms are broken, but presumably the right hand was raised in the attitude of imparting protection, whilst the left held the monastic robe. In their general style, and particularly in the treatment of the drapery with its schematic folds, these images exhibit a close relationship to the Buddha type of Amarāvatī.

The same site yielded two colossal standing figures in royal attire which are believed to represent two ancient monarchs of Ceylon. These popular identifications, however, have no historical value. The one,

preserved in the Colombo Museum, appear to represent scenes from the Buddha legend.

[1] The presence of the horse seems hardly to supply sufficient justification for identifying the figure as Kapila Muni.

measuring 8 feet in height, carved in dolomite but now much weather-worn, is supposed to be King Bhātiyatissa I (*acc.* 19 B.C.); the other, 10 feet high and well-preserved, has been identified as an effigy of Dutthagāmani, the founder of the Mahāthūpa.

The larger statue, however, was found in a ruined shrine which also contained the four colossal Buddha figures noticed above. If these four figures were meant to represent the Buddhas who have appeared in the present *kalpa* we may perhaps assume that the fifth image, in kingly attire, represents the last Buddha of this age who is yet to come, namely, the Bodhisattva Maitreya. The statue popularly identified as King Bhātiyatissa has the hands raised in the attitude of adoration. This lends some support to the assumption that the statue represents, indeed, a royal donor.

A Buddha image of a type different from the standing figures of the Ruanwäli Dāgaba is the colossal statue (8 feet high) carved in very dark granite which is hidden in the forest of Anurādhapura. It shows the Buddha seated in the attitude of meditation with folded legs and the hands resting in the lap. This well-preserved image is a grand work of art in which mental repose is admirably expressed.

The site of the medieval capital of Polonnaruwa is now marked by a large number of secular and religious monuments, several of them of imposing size but all in a more or less far-advanced state of decay. Here, as in Anurādhapura, Tamil invasions are responsible for the ruin of these works of art. Most of the ancient monuments of Polonnaruwa are associated with the great King Parakkama Bāhu (A.D. 1153–86) under whose rule the town reached the zenith of its prosperity. Many of the monuments, including most of the shrines at the Quadrangle as well as the Rankot Vehera, are due to Niśśanka Malla (1187–96), the first ruler of the Kalinga dynasty. In 1215 the throne was usurped by Māgha, the Tamil chief, who during his reign persecuted the Buddhists and despoiled their sanctuaries.

It will be impossible to give here an adequate account of the numerous buildings, the ruins of which extend far to the north from the ancient citadel of Parakkama Bāhu. It may be said that in general the architecture and sculpture of Polonnaruwa are evolved from the art of the earlier capital. This is especially apparent in the two large *stūpas* called Rankot Vehera and Kiri Vehera,[1] which have retained the archaic type of Anurādhapura in a remarkable degree. As regards size, too, the Rankot Vehera may well compete with the gigantic *stūpas* of Dutthagāmani and Vattagāmani Abhaya.

A new class of religious edifices is represented by the two large brick temples known as Jetavanārāma and Thūpārāma. The real name of the former is

[1] The Kiri Vehera, which is northernmost, must be identical with the Damila Thūpa or 'Tamil Tope' built by Parakkama Bāhu. It was so called because Tamil prisoners of war were employed in building it, as stated in the *Mahāvaṃsa* lxxviii. 81.

Lankātilaka, or 'the Ornament of Ceylon'.[1] In their present ruinous condition both these temples are still imposing piles of brickwork bearing the traces of profuse decoration in which the influence of Dravidian architecture is noticeable. The entrance flanked by two lofty pylons is on the east side, so that the gigantic standing Buddha, projecting from the back wall of the sanctum and constructed of plastered brickwork like the whole temple, also faces the rising sun. In the Lankātilaka there are remnants of frescoes, some of which represent *jātakas*[2].

Here, as in most other monuments of Polonnaruwa, the vestibule is ascended by means of an ornamental staircase which is very similar to those of Anurādhapura. In the later capital we find likewise the moonstone and the two guardstones each carved with a Nāga figure which, however, do not reach the degree of artistic excellence attained by the earlier age. On the whole both the architecture and sculpture of Polonnaruwa show a decline in creative power when compared with the artistic productions of Anurādhapura.

Among the works which are most admired at Polonnaruwa we may mention the group of rock-cut images found at Gal Vihāra at the northern extremity of the site.[3] The Nirvāna statue, measuring 46 feet

[1] *Mahāvaṃsa*, lxxviii. 52–4.

[2] Earlier specimens of pictorial art are found at Sigiriya.

[3] It is mentioned in the *Mahāvaṃsa*, lxxviii. 76–8, under the name of Uttarārāma, i.e. 'the Northern Monastery'.

in length, is impressive because of its enormous size but can hardly be regarded as a thing of beauty. The pathos which we might expect in the image of the dying Teacher is completely wanting. The erect statue, likewise hewn out of the rock, at some distance from the head of the recumbent colossus, is thought to represent Ānanda, the favourite disciple of the Buddha. But there is good reason to doubt this identification. From the existing remains it is obvious that the two figures were originally placed in two different shrines and were separated by a partition wall, so that in all probability they were not meant at all to form one group. Possibly the standing figure, too, is in reality a Buddha, although it must be admitted that the absence of the *ushnīsha* and *ūrnā* and the unusual attitude with the arms crossed seem to militate against such an assumption.[1]

A work of far greater merit is the colossal rock-cut image found at the Potgul Monastery, which is popularly believed to represent the great Parakkama Bāhu. There exist, however, serious objections to this identification. The figure with its simple dress, imposing beard, and braided hair, shown in the act

[1] It should be observed that none of the Buddha figures at the Gal Vihāra has now the sign of the *ūrnā*; but as the images were originally plastered and painted we may perhaps assume that it was indicated in paint. As regards the *ushnīsha*, the head of the so-called Ānanda is broken at the top; it is impossible to decide what form it had originally. The hair, however, is arranged in ringlets in the manner of Buddha figures. Cf. *Ceylon Journal of Science*, Section G, vol. ii, p. 15.

of reading a palm-leaf book, can hardly be a royal personage, but has the aspect of a Brahmanical *rishi*. Whether it represents Kapila the ascetic, as supposed by Mr. Bell, or Agastya the sage revered equally in southern India and in Java, it is impossible to decide. Whatever its real meaning may be it is certainly a masterpiece and perhaps the greatest work of art found in Ceylon. It may be questioned whether this rock-cut image which testifies to such a marvellous power of expression does not belong to a much earlier age than the reign of the king whom it is supposed to portray.[1]

[1] S. Paranavitana, 'The Statue at the Potgul Vehera in Polonnaruva' (*Ceylon Journal of Science*, Section G, vol. ii, pp. 229 ff.).

X

The Buddhist Art of Java

IT may seem strange that the greatest monument of the Buddhist religion is not found in India proper where Buddhism originated, but far away in the Isle of Java where it was introduced at a comparatively late date.

When the Chinese pilgrim Fā-hien visited Java on his voyage home from Ceylon to China about A.D. 400, he stated that the number of true believers was very small and that they were outnumbered by the heretics, as he calls them, viz. by the followers of Brahmanism. The statement of the pilgrim is confirmed by epigraphical evidence. The earliest inscriptions which have come to light in the Malay Archipelago are all Brahmanical.

The first Buddhist inscription is dated in the year 700 of the Śaka era, corresponding to A.D. 778. This document, found near the village of Kalasan in central Java, is remarkable for several reasons. It records the construction of a temple dedicated to the goddess Tārā, together with a dwelling for the *bhikshus* (i.e. monks) who know the Vinaya and the Mahāyāna. So it is definitely said here that the sanctuary of Kalasan belonged to that later form of Buddhism which is designated by the name of Mahāyāna or 'the Great Vehicle'.

There is yet another point of great interest in the Kalasan inscription. It says that the temple of Tārā was founded by a king whose name is not mentioned but who is designated as 'the Ornament of the Śailendra Race'. At the time when the inscription was first published nothing was known about this Śailendra race. But since then several epigraphical documents have come to light which have supplied valuable information regarding this mysterious dynasty. We now know that the Śailendras were the rulers of Śrīvijaya, a mighty kingdom comprising Sumatra, Java, and the Malay Peninsula. They were zealous Buddhists and founded sanctuaries not only in their own dominions but even at Nālandā, the famous seat of Buddhist learning in southern Bihār, and at Negapatam on the coast of Coromandel.

There is good reason to assume that the great *stūpa* of Barabudur, too, is a monument due to the piety of the Śailendras. It is true that no record of its foundation has come to light. But according to the best authorities the famous sanctuary of Java must have been raised in the latter half of the eighth century, and it appears that at that time Java was under the influence of the Śailendra kings.

The Barabudur is a most elaborate *stūpa* in its construction and ornamentation and is, in fact, quite unique (Plate 36). Yet there can hardly be any doubt that it is derived from the simple relic-shrines of India. It is built on the top of a hill in the midst of the fertile plains of Kedu enclosed by a number of gigantic volcanoes. The beauty of the surrounding scenery adds greatly to the charm of the mighty monument.

The whole pile is raised on a large basement, but this is partly a later addition. It seems that while the huge *stūpa* was being constructed there were indications that the ponderous fabric was threatening to subside. This must have induced the architects to strengthen the original basement by means of a stone encasement. That such a measure became necessary is greatly to be deplored. Not only was the series of 160 reliefs carved on the original basement and not yet fully completed thus concealed from sight, but the enlargement has moreover emphasized the somewhat squat aspect of the whole structure.

The body of the building consists of a succession of terraces, nine in number, of which the six lower ones are square and the three upper ones circular. Although the former may be roughly described as square it will be seen from the ground-plan that the four sides have doubly recessed corners. This arrangement brings out the contrast between light and shade on the façades of the edifice and at the same time counteracts the preponderance of the horizontal line.

Four flights of steps lead up to the top of the monument, starting from the middle of each of the four sides of the square basement. On each square terrace

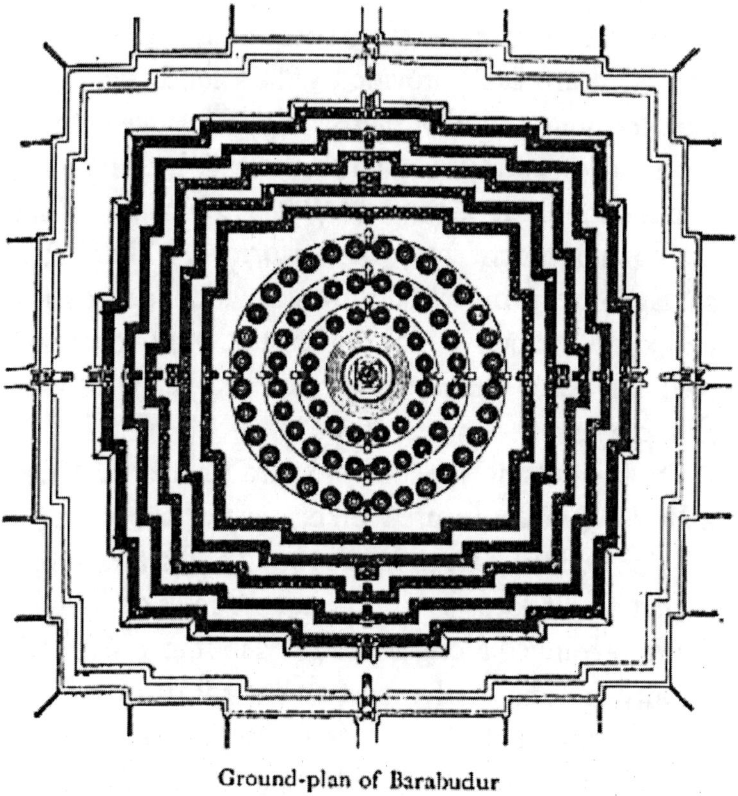

Ground-plan of Barabudur

they pass through a gateway lavishly adorned with sculpture. Most prominent in the decoration of these gateways is the so-called *kāla-makara*, consisting of a lion-head placed in the apex of the arch combined with two *makara*-heads.

The four square terraces succeeding the enlarged basement are each provided with a solid stone rampart forming a kind of balustrade. Thus we get four corridors or passages, open to the sky, by which the circumambulation, the so-called *pradakshinā*, of the sacred monument may be performed. These four passages are profusely decorated with long rows of sculptured panels which cover not only the main wall but also the inner surface of the balustrade (Plate 37).

On the outside the four balustrades are provided with rows of sculptured niches each harbouring a life-size Buddha carved in the round and seated cross-legged on his lotus-seat. These long rows of Buddha figures arranged along the façades in impressive uniformity are one of the most striking features of the whole monument. On closer inspection, however, it will be seen that these Buddha images are not quite identical. They differ in one respect, namely, the *mudrā*.

It has long been recognized that the four classes of Buddha statues arranged along the four façades of the Barabudur, and each distinguished by a particular *mudrā*, must represent the four Dhyāni-Buddhas which are associated with the four cardinal points. They are Akshobhya whose gesture is that of touching the earth (*bhūmisparśa-mudrā*) on the east, Ratnasambhava whose gesture expresses bounty (*varada-mudrā*) on the south, Amitābha seated in meditation (*dhyāna-mudrā*) on the west, and Amoghasiddha who imparts protection (*abhaya-mudrā*) on the north (Plate 38). Each of these four Dhyāni-Buddhas is represented by no less than 92 statues enshrined in as many niches which are arranged in four horizontal rows along the respective façades. Besides this there is an upper row of Buddha figures 64 times repeated and placed along the edge of the highest square terrace. These all exhibit the attitude of argumentation (*vitarka-mudrā*) and must portray the fifth Dhyāni-Buddha, named Vairochana, who might be called the Buddha of the Zenith. On each façade the total number of enshrined Buddha figures consequently amounts to 108 which has ever been considered an auspicious number in India.

The six square terraces, as has been noted, are surmounted by three more which are circular in shape. It is highly remarkable that whereas the former are profusely decorated the superstructure is void of all ornament. This contrast is perhaps intentional. The lower terraces, it has been surmised, represent the phenomenal world; but when the pilgrim has ascended to the upper platforms he has left the world of senses behind and has now reached the spiritual spheres where he may devote himself to meditation.

This much is certain that the three circular terraces are severely plain. They are beset with small *dāgabas* arranged in three concentric circles and numbering 32, 24, and 16 respectively, so that their total number amounts to 72. These 72 *dāgabas* are of a type unknown in other parts of the Buddhist world. Instead of being solid domes they present the appearance of perforated, bell-shaped domes each enshrining a Buddha image seated in the attitude of preaching (*dharmachakra-mudrā*). Here we have apparently a sixth Dhyāni-Buddha, who is considered by some schools to be the highest of all and who is identified, in fact, with the supreme deity. His name is Vajrasattva.

The uppermost circular terrace is occupied by a large-sized *dāgaba*, measuring 52 feet in diameter, which crowns the whole monument. We recognize in it the form of the early hemispherical *stūpa* of India.

From an artistic point of view the Barabudur is invaluable on account of its sculptures which are unsurpassed in the East for their profusion and beauty. Both the main walls and the balustrades all along the four passages are covered with continuous rows of sculptured panels. It has been calculated that there are nearly 1,500 such panels and that the sculptures of the Barabudur, if placed side by side, would extend for three miles. But it is especially owing to their aesthetic value that these sculptures are remarkable. They are, of course, not all of equal merit but most of them are far above the average and several are real masterpieces. The artists who produced these wonderful sculptures show very great skill in rendering the human figure. The attitude of the principal personages is graceful and noble. Equal ability is shown in depicting accessories such as buildings, and forest scenery, which latter is invariably enlivened by various animals. The elephants and monkeys especially, are admirably characterized.

The identification of the sculptured panels has proved a task of considerable difficulty. This is due to various causes. The elongated form of the panels induced the sculptors to fill most of the space with numerous figures of attendants and with accessories which are apt to obscure the real subject of the sculpture. The artist renders types but not individuals. Bearded figures in scanty dress are Brahmans; personages wearing a rich attire and abundant ornaments are kings, princes, or nobles, but may also be *devas*. No attempt, however, is made to characterize a special personage either by his facial expression, hairdress, or garments. There is a marked tendency to evade the rendering of violent scenes except when such subjects were unavoidable, as is the case with several reliefs on the basement partly portraying the punishments in hell.

Notwithstanding these difficulties the work of interpretation has made considerable progress, thanks to the efforts of several scholars versed in Buddhist lore. It is a point of primary importance that the sculptors who decorated the great *stūpa* have closely followed certain sacred Sanskrit texts which no doubt enjoyed great repute in their days. Several of these texts have now been identified.

Let us commence our review with the reliefs on the basement which are now concealed. On their discovery by Dr. J. W. Yzerman in 1885 it was recognized at once that most of these panels referred to the retribution of good and evil deeds. In particular the wicked acts and the corresponding torments awaiting the sinner after death were unmistakable. It was the distinguished French orientalist, M. Sylvain Lévi, who recognized in these sculptures illustrations of the *Karmavibhanga*, a work describing the retribution of acts (*karman*).

Along the main wall of the first gallery there runs a double row each consisting of 120 panels. The upper row illustrates a famous Sanskrit text, the *Lalitavistara*, which relates in glowing language the life-story of the Buddha up to the first sermon at Benares. In the lower row of panels another French scholar, M. Alfred Foucher, has recognized a number of *avadānas* or edifying tales.

The reliefs which are arranged along the balustrades of the first and second passages show a large number of *jātakas*. The first set of thirty-four birth stories here illustrated are the same as those described in very noble language in another famous Sanskrit work, the *Jātakamālā*.

The series of the Buddha legend includes some of the finest specimens of Indo-Javanese sculpture, in which the serene spirit of Buddhism is expressed in a marvellous manner. We reproduce two specimens; the one shows the Bodhisattva practising austerities in the wilderness in the company of the five Brahmanical anchorites, the other represents him crossing the river Nairanjanā previous to his Enlightenment while divine beings are paying him homage (Plate 39).

The reliefs of the second, third, and fourth galleries, though on the whole highly decorative, are somewhat monotonous when compared with those of the first passage. Professor N. J. Krom has established beyond doubt that the panels arranged along the main wall of the second passage are meant to visualize the contents of the *Gandavyūha*. This work describes the wanderings of the Bodhisattva Sudhana in search of Supreme Wisdom. In his quest he visits a great number of wise men, gods, and Bodhisattvas, including Manjuśrī, Maitreya, and Samantabhadra. It would seem that this edifying subject is continued on the main walls of the third and fourth passages, Maitreya being conspicuous in the series of the third and Samantabhadra in those of the fourth gallery.

If we now attempt to unravel the mystery of this

great monument of the Mahāyāna, as it is revealed in its rows of illustrative reliefs, we would summarize the result as follows. The pilgrim, on approaching the sacred shrine, will first of all be made to realize the inexorable law of *karman* which originally was visualized in the now hidden panels of the basement. When ascending the flight of steps on the east side and commencing the circumambulation of the first gallery, he will behold in what manner the Master, after having prepared himself for his great task in a succession of hundreds of lives, descended on the earth for the last time to be born as the Śākya prince who realized the vanity of all phenomena and vanquished the demon of lust to become the Saviour from transmigration and transitory existence. When next the pilgrim betakes himself to the farther galleries he will witness the search for the highest truth revealed by the great Bodhisattvas of the Mahāyāna. When at last he has reached the summit of the *stūpa* the phenomenal world vanishes from his sight and he is transported into the sphere of mere thought.

It will be impossible here to enter on a detailed aesthetic discussion of the reliefs of Barabudur. We wish, however, to point out that these sculptures are different from anything found in India. Nowhere do we find a sculptural illustration of Buddhist lore and doctrine so marvellous in its extent and detail. Also, they are distinguished by a definite style in which mental repose is expressed in forms of singular gracefulness. It deserves notice that the portrayal of human society, animal life, and vegetation is distinctly Indonesian.

Before leaving the Barabudur a few words may be added about the later history of the great *stūpa*. When on the introduction of Islām in the Malay Archipelago Buddhist worship ceased, the Barabudur must have fallen into decay, and in the course of time it was buried under its own debris and covered by a tropical vegetation. In 1814 it was noticed by Sir Stamford Raffles who ordered it to be excavated and surveyed. In the years 1907–11 extensive measures for its preservation were carried out under the able superintendence of Lieut.-Colonel T. van Erp, R.E. The monument is now entrusted to the care of the Archaeological Survey of Netherlands India. A beautifully illustrated monograph by Dr. N. J. Krom and Lieut.-Colonel T. van Erp, containing a full account both of the sculpture and architecture of the great monument, was published in the years 1920 and 1931 at the cost of the Government.

Besides the Barabudur, Javanese Buddhism has produced a considerable number of shrines, much smaller in size and fame but still remarkable on account of their architecture and sculptural decoration. We must restrict ourselves to a brief survey of the principal among these edifices.

Only a few miles from the Barabudur there are two Buddhist temples which must have been closely connected with the great *stūpa* and probably belong to the same period. The larger one, known by the name of Chandi Mendut, consists of a square shrine with recessed corners raised on a large basement of the same shape which is ascended by means of a flight of steps. The whole surface of the edifice is covered with exquisite sculptures. The walls of the temple proper show graceful figures of Bodhisattvas and goddesses; the two walls enclosing the staircase exhibit a number of animal fables, here probably meant for *jātakas*, which are continued all along the surface of the basement.

The vestibule leading to the sanctum is decorated with two graceful panels representing the one the god of wealth, the other the goddess of fertility. The spacious cella enshrines three well-preserved stone statues of imposing size and great beauty. The central one is a monolith of 9 feet in height, representing Buddha seated in the European fashion and in the act of preaching his first sermon, as is evident from the wheel and deer symbol on the pedestal. The two attendant images are Bodhisattvas. The one seated to the right of the Buddha is Avalokiteśvara carrying the figurine of his spiritual father Amitābha in his head-dress. The other seems to portray Manjuśrī.

The smaller temple, known as Chandi Pawon, is likewise a square structure raised on a large basement. The cluster of small dāgabas on the roof clearly demonstrates the connexion of this graceful little shrine with Buddhism. On account of the sculptures in which the wishing-tree and treasure-vase are most prominent it has been conjectured that it was dedicated to Kubera, the god of wealth. However incongruous with the spirit of Buddhism, images of this deity have actually been found in Buddhist convents and temples in India.

A very important group of monuments of the Hindu period is found near the village of Prambanan to the east of Jogyakarta. Most prominent are the three lofty temples dedicated to the three great gods of Hinduism—Brahmā, Vishnu, and Śiva—the last-mentioned god occupying the central and principal place.

But among the numberless ruined shrines scattered over the plains of Prambanan there are several pertaining to Buddhism. There is the profusely decorated Chandi Kalasan which in all probability is identical with the temple of Tārā, the foundation of which by a ruler of the Śailendra dynasty is recorded in a Sanskrit inscription.[1] There is the triple shrine, called Chandi Sari, and the large group of graceful little temples known by the name of Chandi Sewu.

Whereas all the buildings so far described belong to central Java and represent the classical period of

[1] Cf. above, pp. 90 f.

Hindu-Javanese architecture, a later phase of this art is represented by a considerable number of monuments which are found exclusively in the eastern part of the island. These edifices, in the arrangement and decoration of which the indigenous art of Indonesia asserts itself and Hindu influence recedes, are mostly dedicated to Brahmanical deities but include a few which belong to the Buddhist religion. In several instances the temple is at the same time a sepulchral monument, as it served the purpose of preserving the ashes of some Javanese king or queen, who after his or her death was supposed to have been absorbed by the deity to whom the shrine was dedicated. The image of the god or goddess enshrined in the temple was at the same time the statue of the king or queen whose remains had been buried beneath the icon, which indeed was meant to show the features of the deceased personage.

It is not a little curious that the same king was sometimes identified both with a Brahmanical and a Buddhist divinity. This was the case with King Vishnuvardhana who, after his death in A.D. 1268, was worshipped as a Śiva image and as a Buddhist image at the same time, as is stated in the Old-Javanese chronicle. There can be little doubt that the Buddhist effigy of the deceased king is identical with the image of Amoghapāśa, a form of the Bodhisattva Avalokiteśvara which was once enshrined in the Chandi Jago near the town of Malang. The stone image of the Bodhisattva as well as those of the subsidiary deities (the name of each is inscribed in Nāgarī letters on the statue) still retain a pronounced Indian impress. The sculptural decoration of the temple, on the contrary, is wholly Indonesian in character.

Bibliography[1]

GENERAL

J. FERGUSSON, *History of Indian and Eastern Architecture.* London 1876. Second edition revised by J. Burgess, 2 vols. London 1910.

Tree and Serpent Worship. 1868. Second edition 1873.

ALBERT GRÜNWEDEL, *Buddhistische Kunst in Indien.* Berlin 1893. Reprinted 1900. English edition by J. Burgess, London 1901. New edition by E. Waldschmidt, Berlin 1932.

VINCENT A. SMITH, *A History of Fine Art in India and Ceylon from the earliest times to the present day.* Oxford 1911. Second edition revised by K. de B. Codrington, Oxford 1930.

A. FOUCHER, *The Beginnings of Buddhist Art and other Essays on Indian and Central Asian Archaeology.* Paris–London 1917.

E. B. HAVELL, *Indian Sculpture and Painting.* London 1908. Second edition, London 1928.

Cambridge History of India. Vol. i, *Ancient India,* ed. by E. J. Rapson. Cambridge 1922. (Chapter xxvi, *The Monuments of Ancient India,* by Sir J. H. Marshall.)

K. de B. CODRINGTON, *Ancient India.* London 1926.

A. K. COOMARASWAMY, *A History of Indian and Indonesian Art.* London 1927.

LUDWIG BACHHOFER, *Die frühindische Plastik.* Munich 1929. (English translation, Paris 1929.)

STELLA KRAMRISCH, *Indian Sculpture. The Heritage of India Series.* Calcutta 1933.

BHARHUT, SĀNCHI, BODH GAYĀ

A. CUNNINGHAM, *The Stūpa of Bharhut.* London 1879.

Mahābodhi, or the Great Buddhist Temple at Buddhagayā. London 1892.

[1] This Bibliography is not meant to be exhaustive; it contains only the titles of the principal books of reference.

A. FOUCHER, *Les Représentations de jātakas sur les bas-reliefs de Bharhut*. Paris 1908.

La Porte orientale de Sanchi. Paris 1910.

JOHN MARSHALL, *A Guide to Sanchi*. Calcutta 1918.

ANANDA K. COOMARASWAMY, *La Sculpture de Bodh Gayā* (*Ars Asiatica*, vol. xviii). Paris 1935.

B. BARUA, *Barhut* (Indian Research Institute Publications, Fine Arts Series, No. 2). Calcutta 1934.

GANDHĀRA, MATHURĀ, AMARĀVATĪ

A. FOUCHER, *L'Art gréco-bouddhique du Gandhāra*. 2 tomes. Paris 1905–18.

JOHN MARSHALL, *A Guide to Taxila*. Calcutta 1918. Second edition 1921.

D. B. SPOONER, *Handbook to the sculptures in the Peshawar Museum*. Calcutta 1909. Revised edition by H. Hargreaves. Calcutta 1930.

J. PH. VOGEL, *Catalogue of the Archaeological Museum at Mathurā*. Allahabad 1910.

La Sculpture de Mathurā (*Ars Asiatica*, vol. xv). Paris 1930.

J. BURGESS, *Report on the Amarāvatī and Jaggayyapeta Buddhist Stūpas*. London 1887.

A. FOUCHER, 'Les Sculptures d'Amarāvatī'. *Revue des Arts Asiatiques*, vol. v, 1928.

CAVE-TEMPLES

J. FERGUSSON AND J. BURGESS, *The Cave-Temples of India*. London 1880.

J. BURGESS, *Notes on the Bauddha Rock-Temples at Ajanta*. Bombay 1879.

Report on the Buddhist Cave Temples and their Inscriptions. London 1883.

Report on the Elura Cave-Temples. London 1883.

J. GRIFFITHS, *The Paintings in the Buddhist Cave-Temples at Ajanta*. 2 vols. London 1896.

LADY HERRINGHAM, *The Ajanta Frescoes*. London 1915.

A. FOUCHER, *Rapport préliminaire sur l'interprétation des peintures et sculptures.* Bombay 1920.

JOHN MARSHALL, ETC. *The Bagh Caves in the Gwalior State.* London 1927.

V. GOLOUBEW, *Documents pour servir à l'étude d'Ajanta. Les Peintures de la première grotte* (*Ars Asiatica*, x). Paris–Brussels 1927.

G. YAZDANI, *Ajanta. The Colour and Monochrome Reproduction of the Ajanta Frescoes based on Photography.* Parts I–II. London 1930–3.

GUPTA AND LATER

D. R. SAHNI, *Catalogue of the Museum of Archaeology at Sārnāth.* Calcutta 1914.

J. C. FRENCH, *The Art of the Pal Empire.* London 1928.

A. FOUCHER, *Étude sur l'iconographie bouddhique de l'Inde.* Paris 1900–5.

BENOYTOSH BHATTACHARYYA, *The Indian Buddhist Iconography.* London 1924.

STELLA KRAMRISCH, *Pāla and Sena Sculpture.* (Rūpam no. 40.) Calcutta 1930.

R. D. BANERJI, 'Eastern Indian School of Mediaeval Sculpture', *Archaeological Survey of India, N.I.S.*, vol. xlvii. Delhi 1933.

A. J. BERNET KEMPERS, *The Bronzes of Nālandā and Hindu-Javanese Art.* Leyden 1933.

CEYLON

J. G. SMITHER, *Architectural Remains, Anuradhapura, Ceylon.* London 1896 (?)

HENRY W. CAVE, *The Ruined Cities of Ceylon.* London 1897.

H. PARKER, *Ancient Ceylon.* London 1909.

G. E. MITTON, *The Lost Cities of Ceylon.* London 1916.

A. M. HOCART, *The Temple of the Tooth in Kandy.* London 1931.

A. M. HOCART AND S. PARANAVITANA's contributions to the *Ceylon Journal of Science*, Section G, vols. i–ii, 1924–33.

JAVA

J. L. A. BRANDES, *Tjandi Djago*. The Hague–Batavia 1904.

N. J. KROM, *Inleiding tot de Hindoe-Javaansche kunst*. The Hague 1920. Second edition, revised, 1923.

N. J. KROM AND T. VAN ERP, *Beschrijving van Barabudur*. Vol. i, *Archaeologische beschrijving*, The Hague 1920; vol. ii, *Bouwkundige beschrijving*, 1931. An English translation of vol. i was published in 1927.

N. J. KROM, *The Life of Buddha on the Stūpa of Barabudur according to the Lalitavistara Text*. The Hague 1926.

M. P. VERNEUIL, *L'Art à Java, Les temples de la période classique indo-javanaise*. Paris–Brussels 1927.

PAUL MUS, *Barabudur. Les Origines du stūpa et la transmigration*, (*Bulletin de l'École Française d'Extrême-Orient*, vols. xxxii–xxxiii). Hanoi, 1933–4.

Index

[1] The term *Dhyāni-Buddha*, used for the sake of convenience, is not found in Buddhist writings. Cf. E. J. Thomas, *History of Buddhist Thought* (1933), p. 248.

PLATES

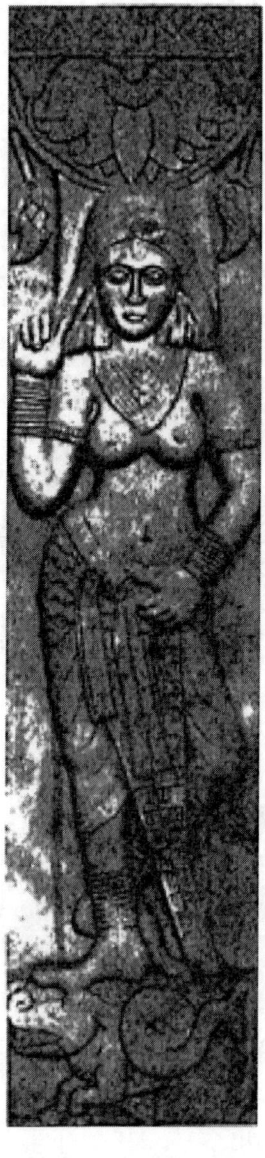

Pl. 2. Railing-pillar with Yakshinī Figure from Bharhut. Indian Museum, Calcutta.

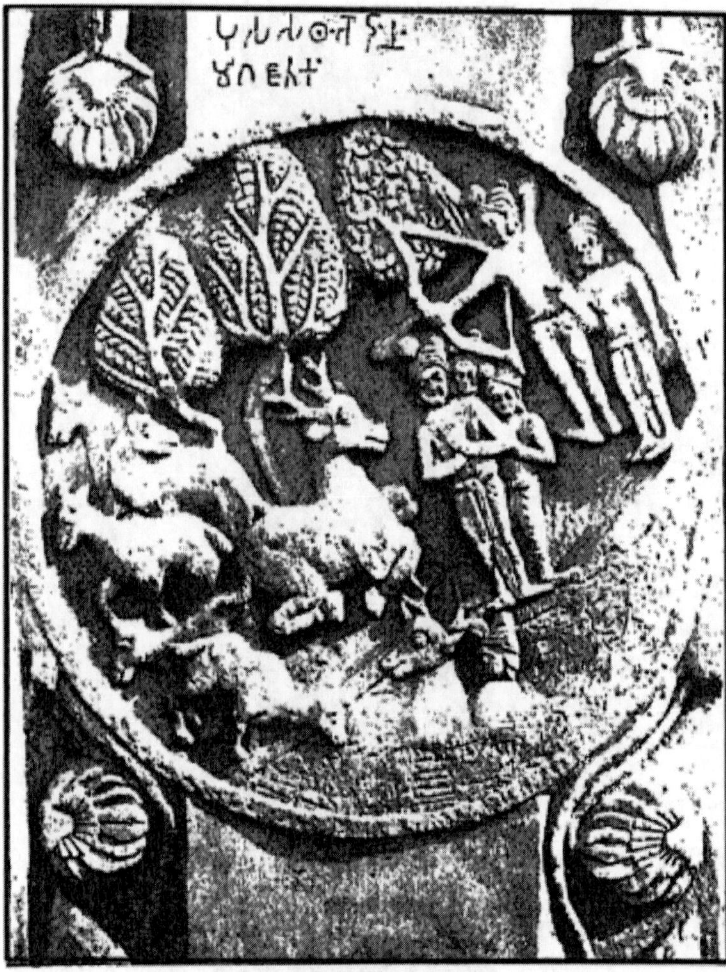

Pl. 3. Ruru-Jātaka on Railing-pillar from Bharhut. Indian Museum, Calcutta.

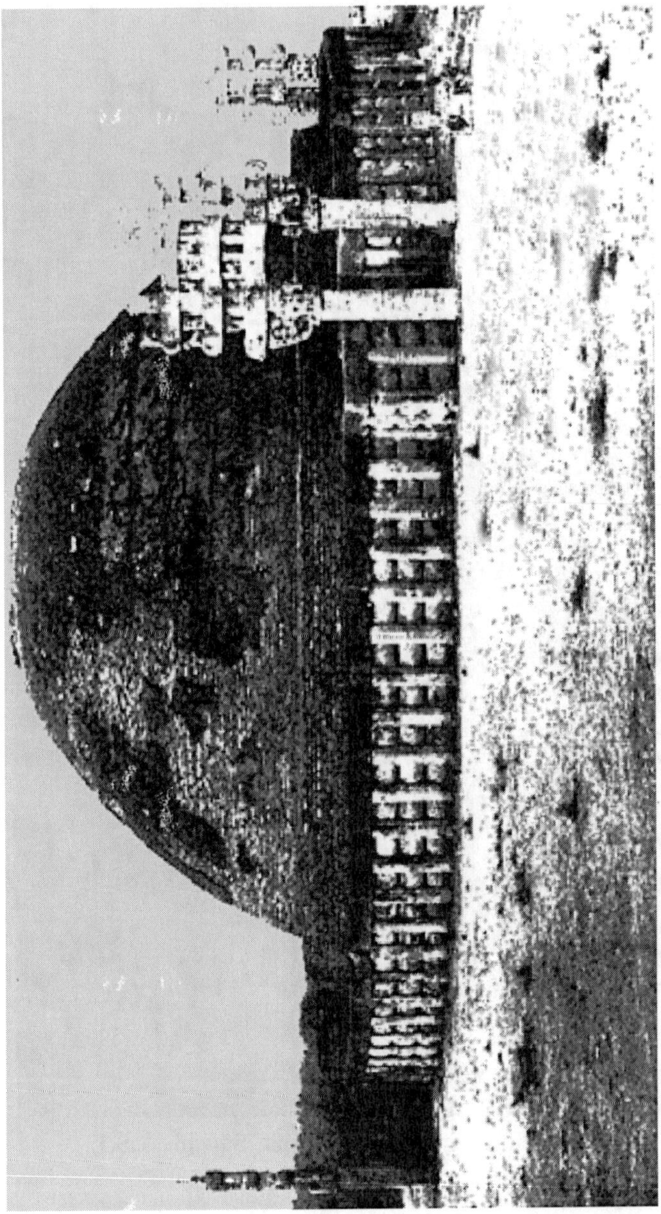

Pl. 4. Great Stūpa of Sānchi from North-East. A.S.I.

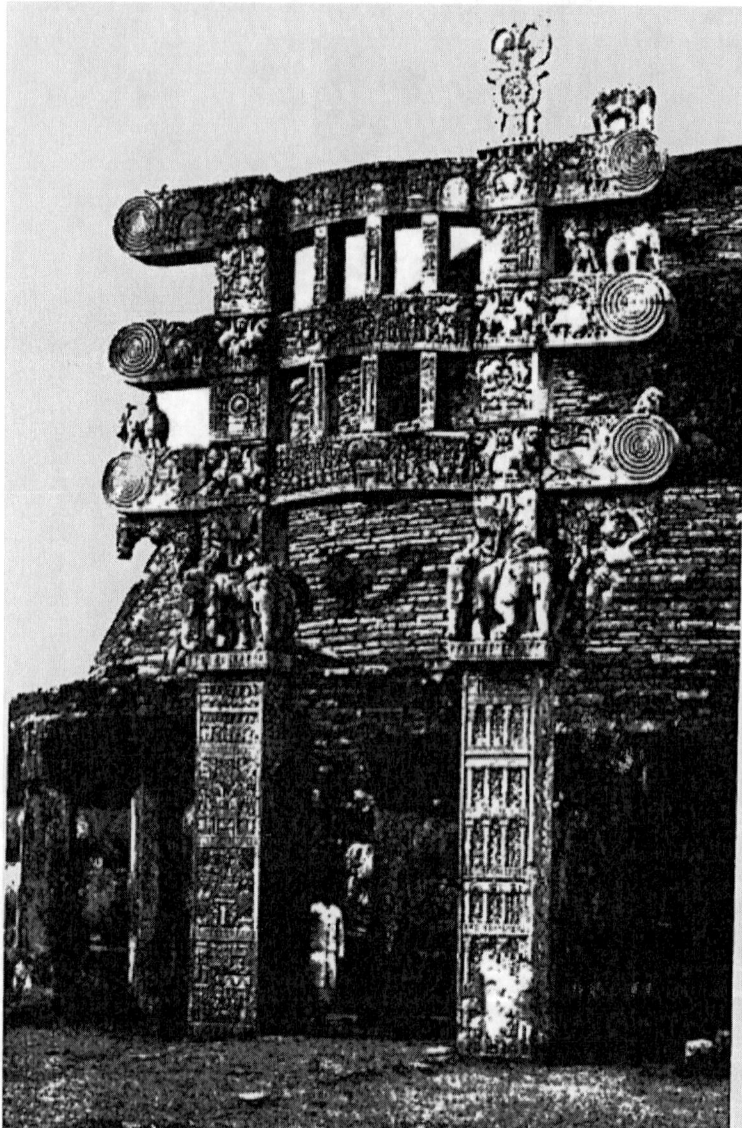

Pl. 5. East Gateway of Great Stūpa, Sānchi. A.S.I.

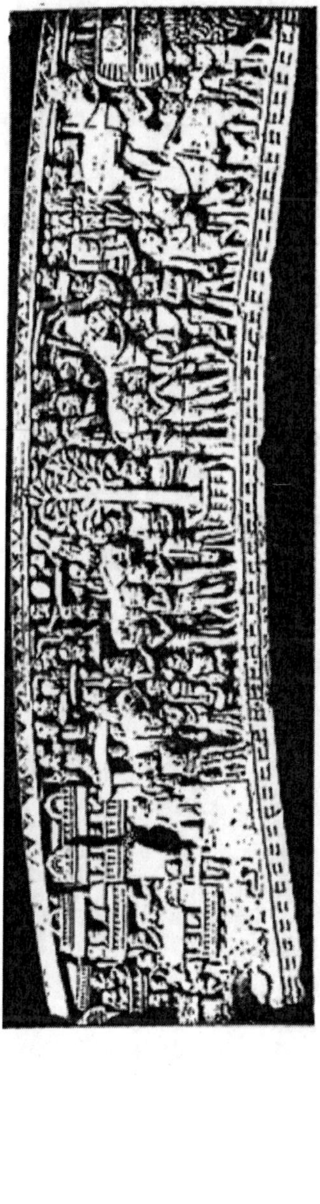

Pl. 6. a. The Great Departure from Kapilavastu, Sānchi. A.S.I.

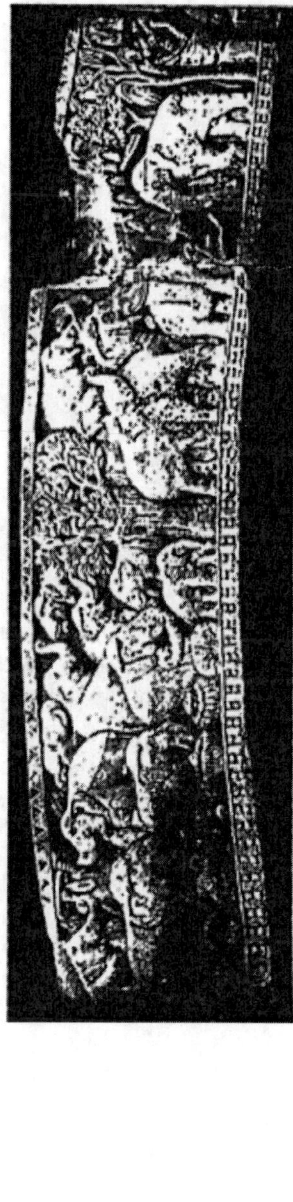

b. Shaddanta-Jātaka, Sānchi. A.S.I.

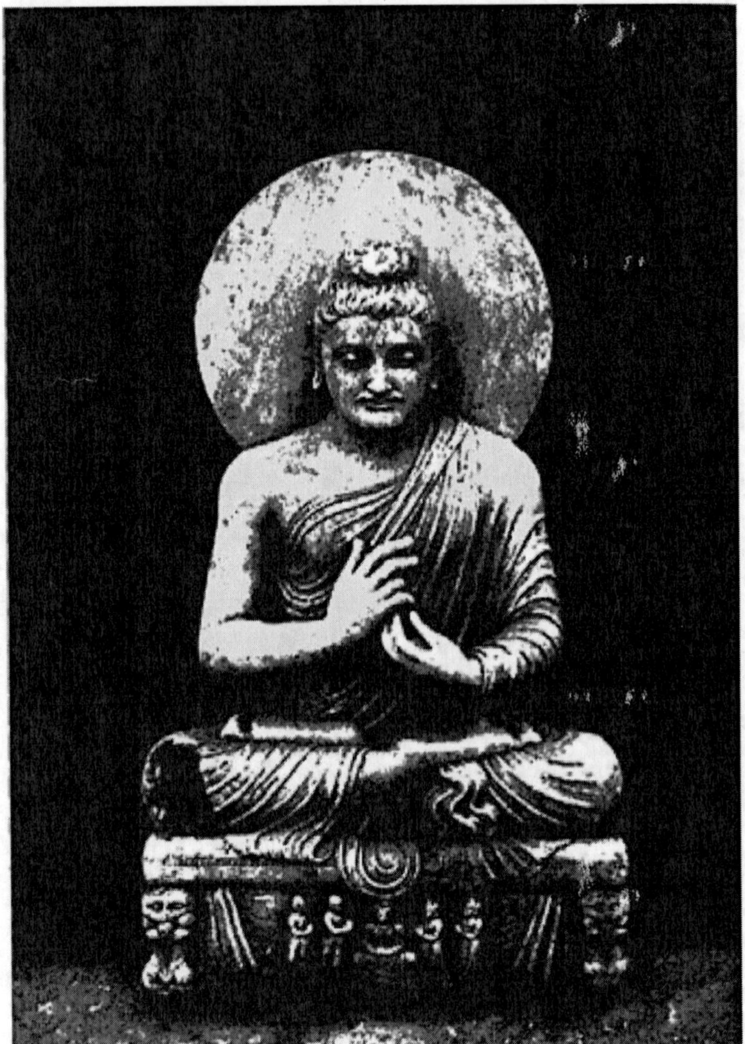

**Pl. 7. Graeco-Buddhist Image of Buddha.
Peshawar Museum**

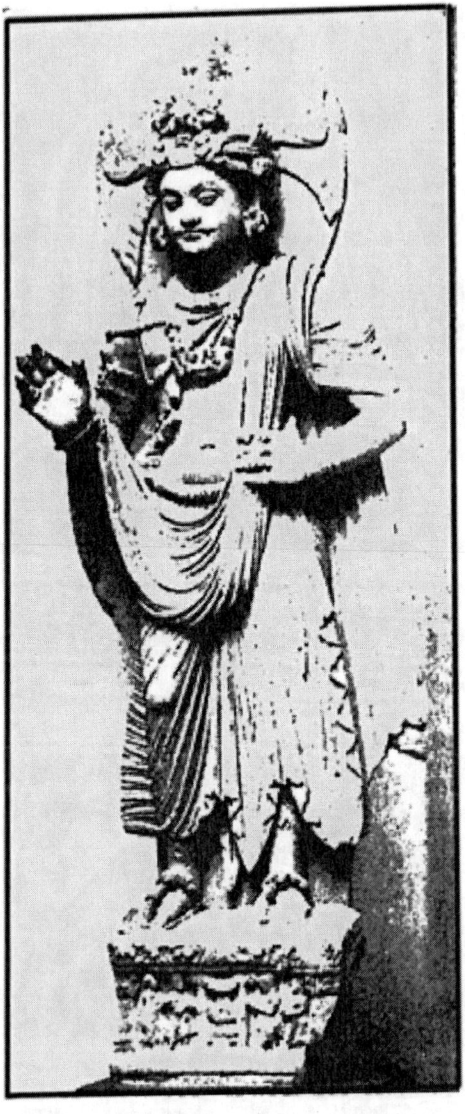

Pl.8. Graeco-Buddhist Image of Bodhisattva from Shāhāz Garhī. Musée du Louvre, Paris.

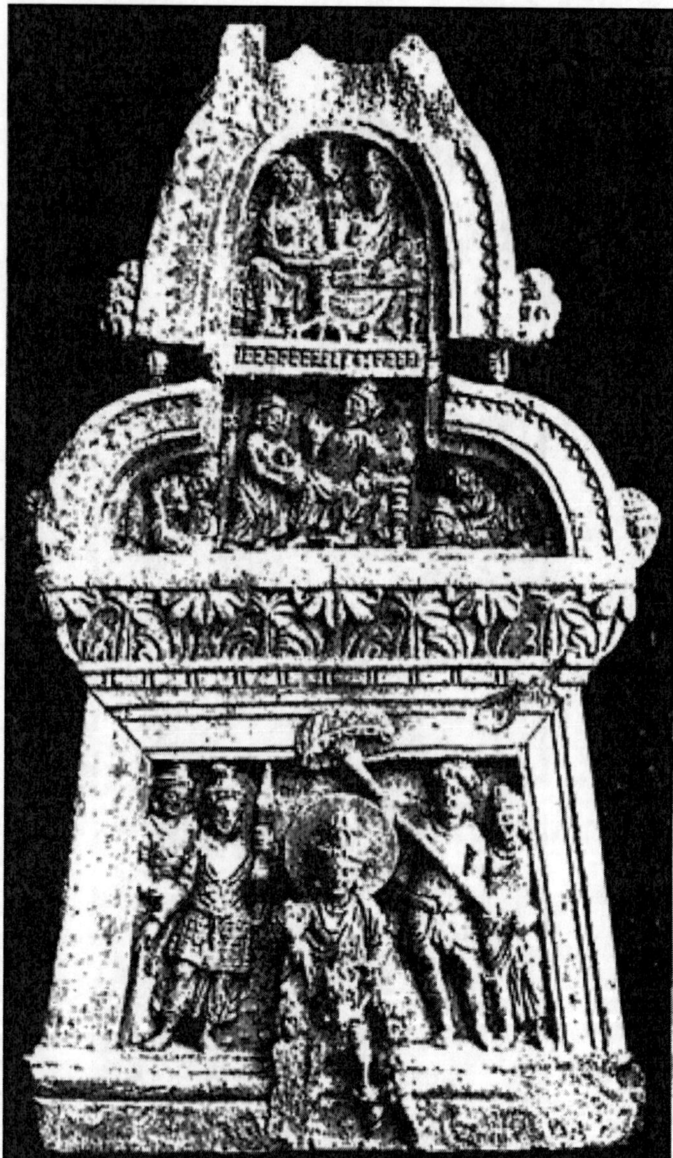

Pl.9. Graeco-Buddhist Relief: The Great Departure from Kapilavastu.

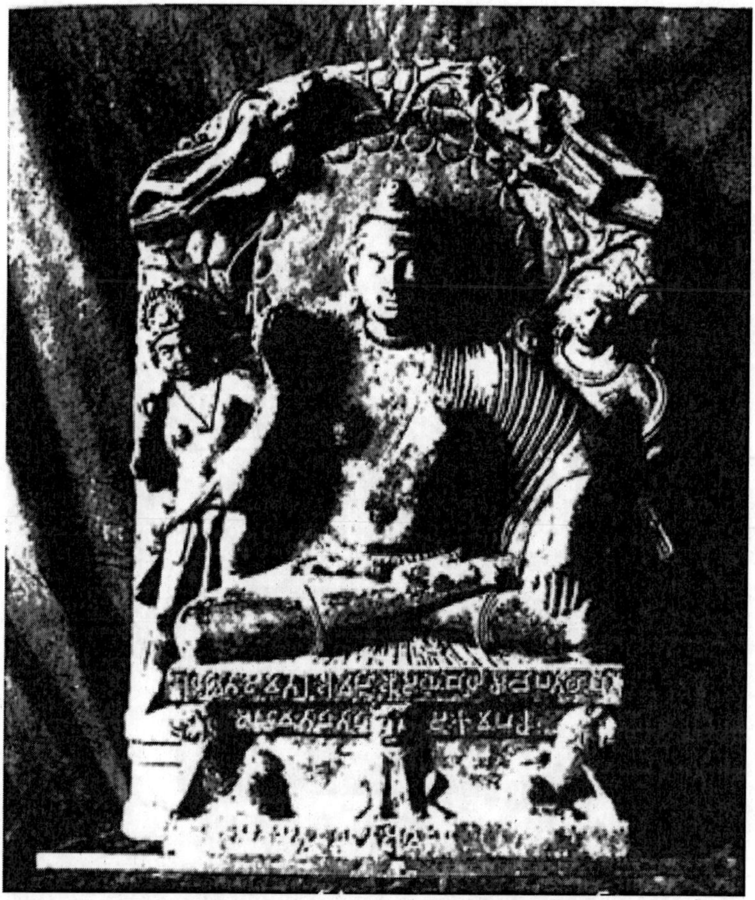

Pl. 10. Buddha Image from the Katrā at Mathurā. Curzon Museum, Mathurā.

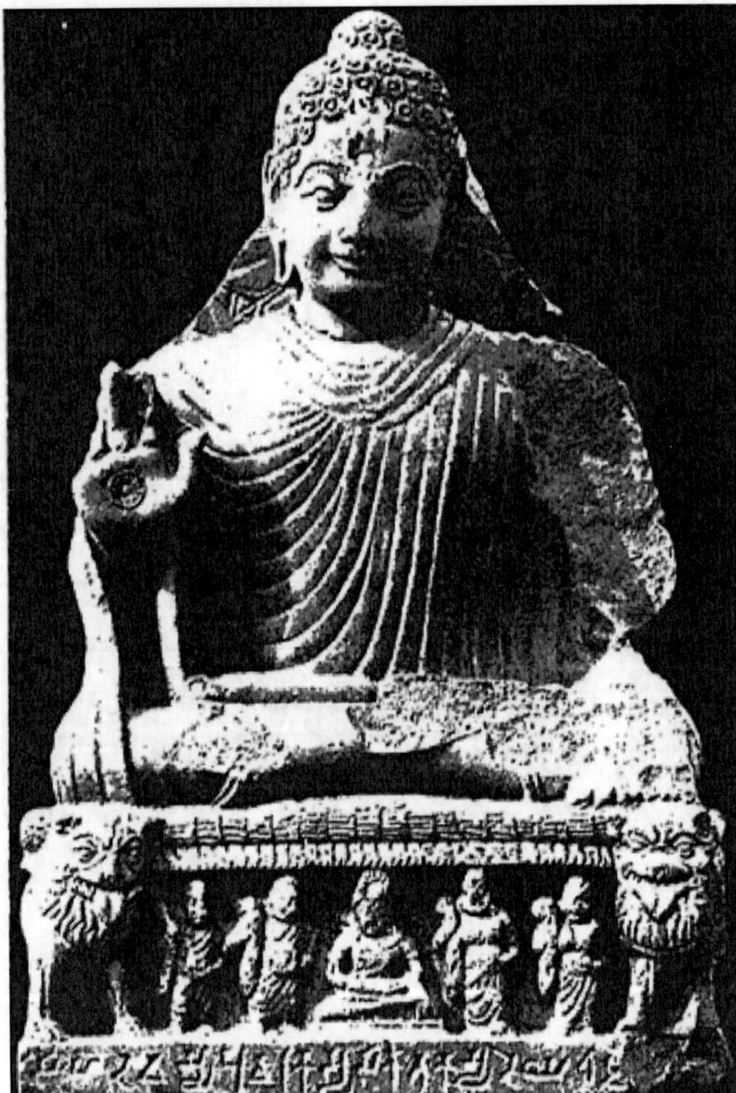

Pl. 11. Buddha Statuette from the Jetavana, Śrāvastī. Provincial Museum, Lucknow.

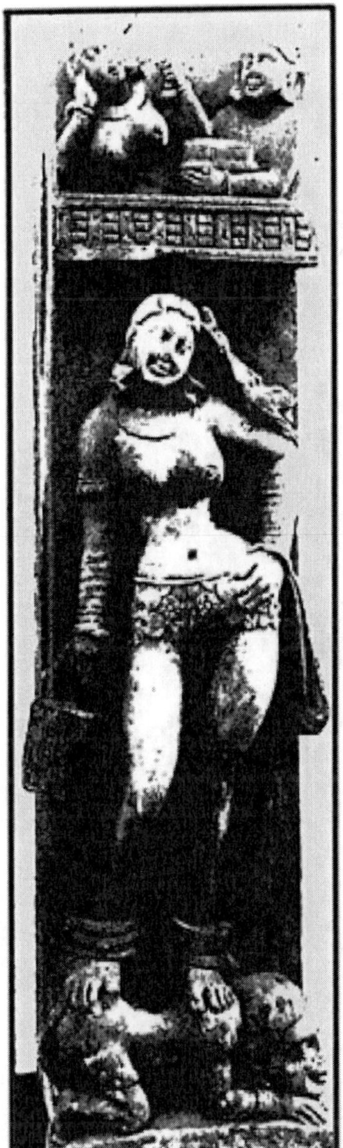

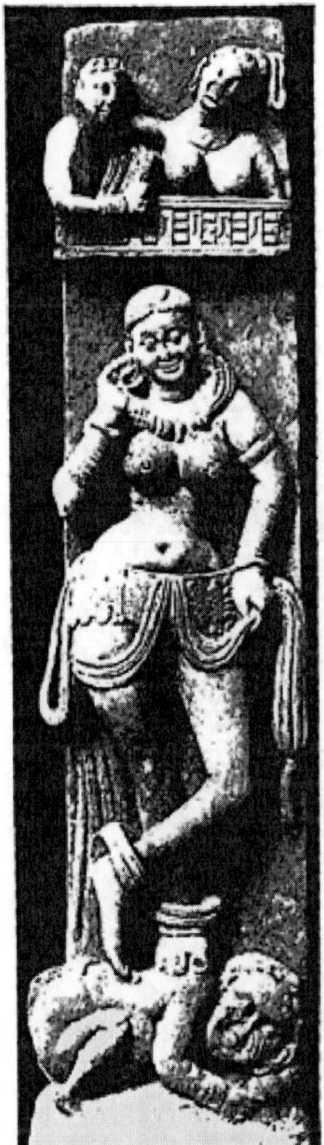

Pl. 12. Railing-Pillars with Female Figures from Bhūtesar, Mathurā.

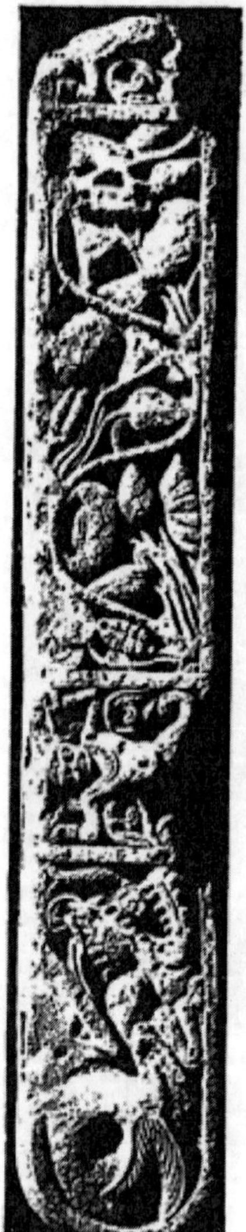

Pl. 13. a. Torana Architrave with Makara and Triton from Mathurā. Provincial Museum, Luknow.

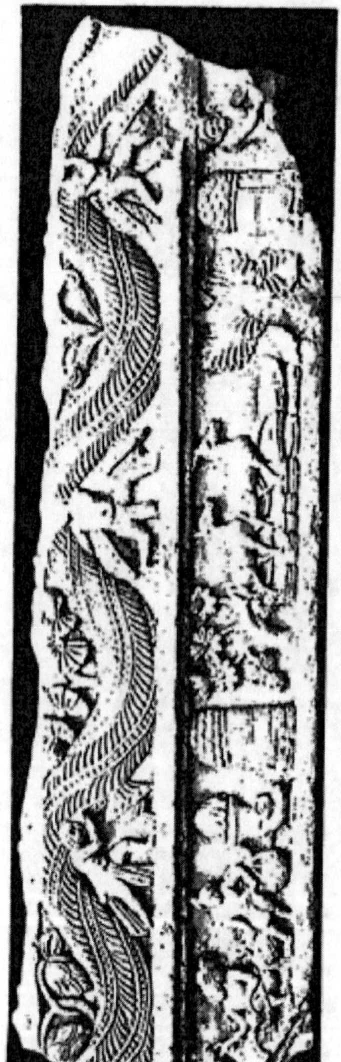

b. Relief with Garland-Bearers and Jātakas from Mathurā. Curzon Museum, Mathurā. A.S.I.

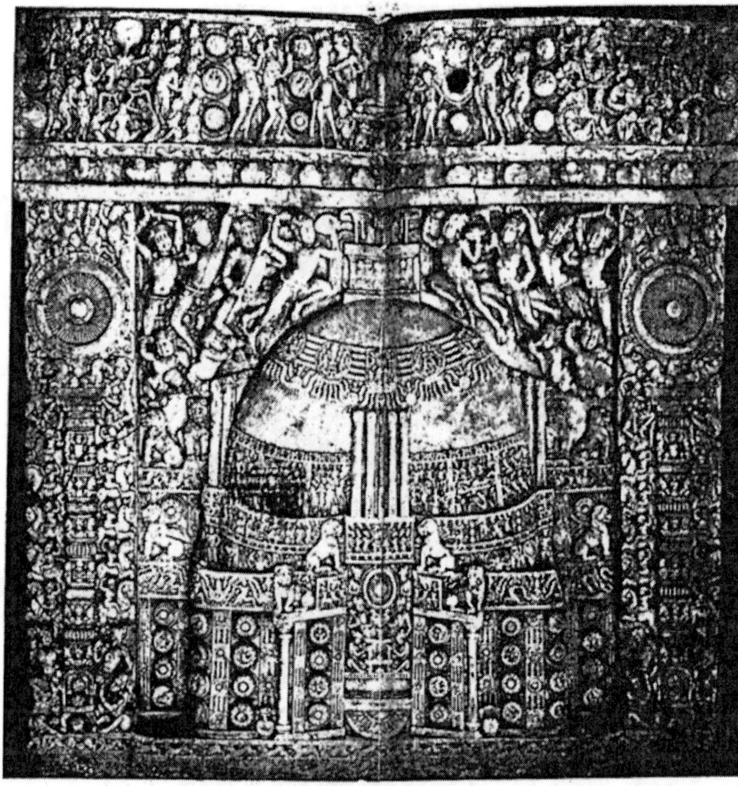

**Pl. 14. Relief from Amarāvatī.
Madras Museum.**

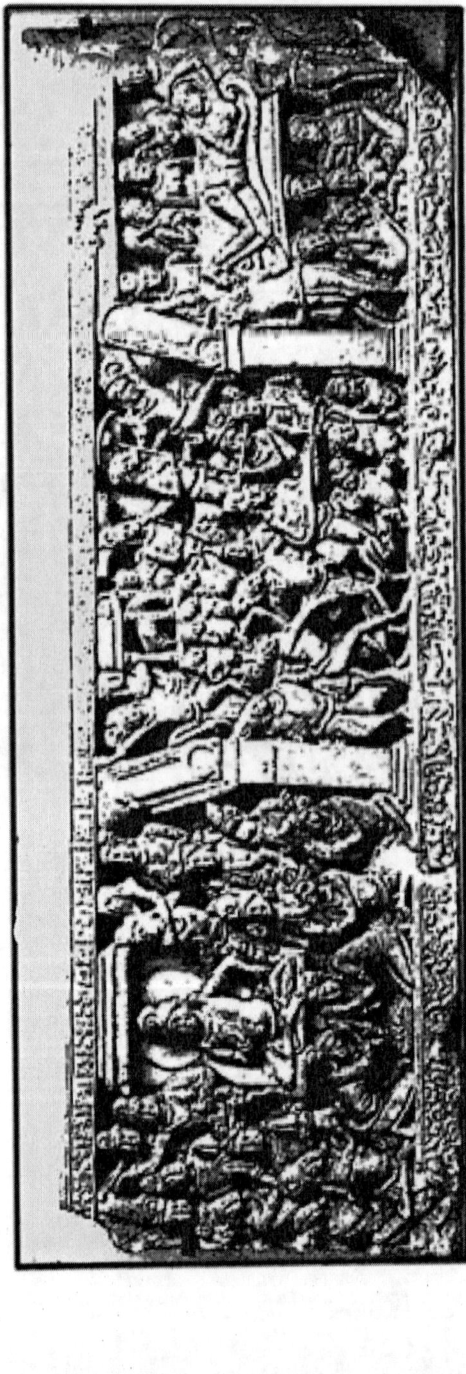

Pl. 15. The Descent of the Bodhisattva, Amarāvatī. Indian Museum, Calcutta.

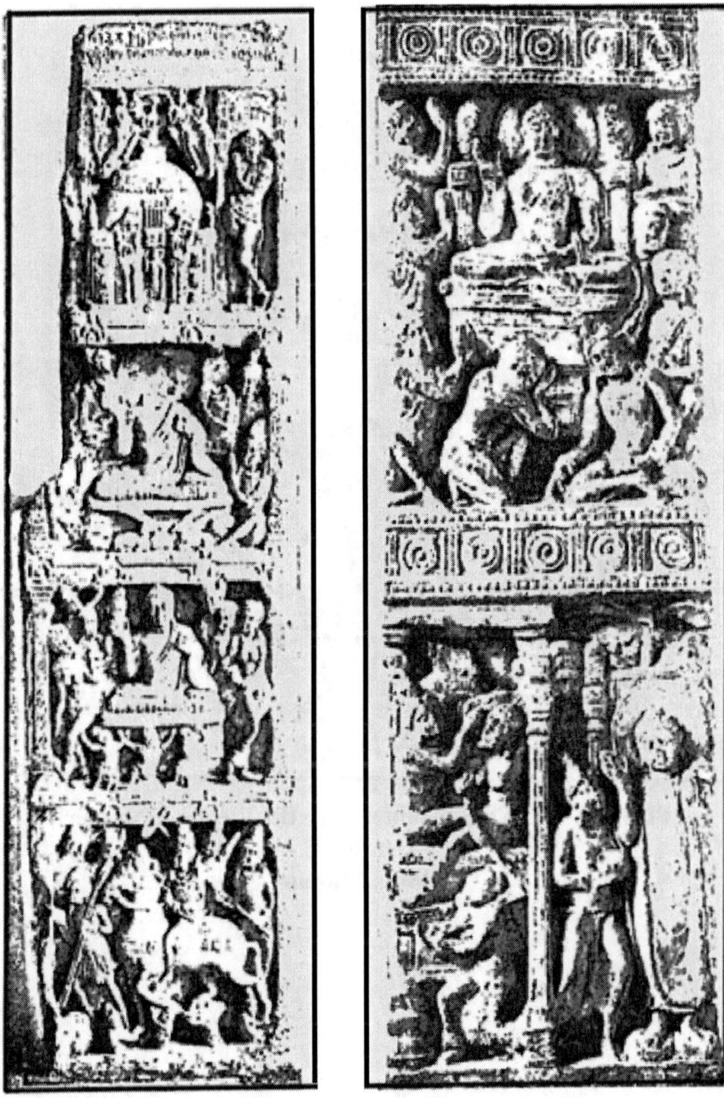

a b

Pl. 16. a. The Four Principal Moments of the Buddha Legend, Amarāvatī.
b. The Conversion of Nanda, Amarāvatī.
Madras Museum.

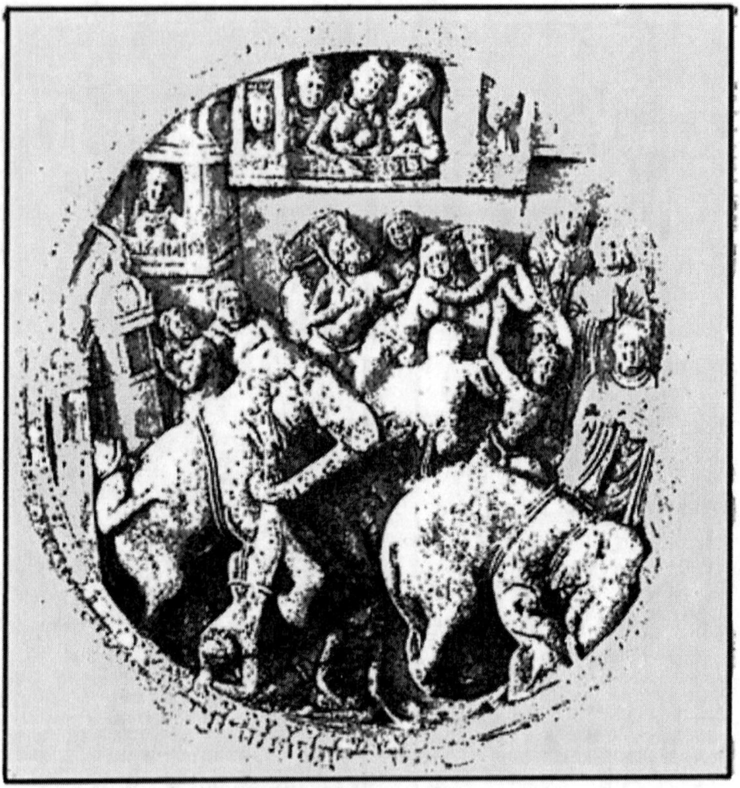

Pl. 17. Buddha's Encounter with the Elephant Nālāgiri, Amarāvatī. Madras Museum.

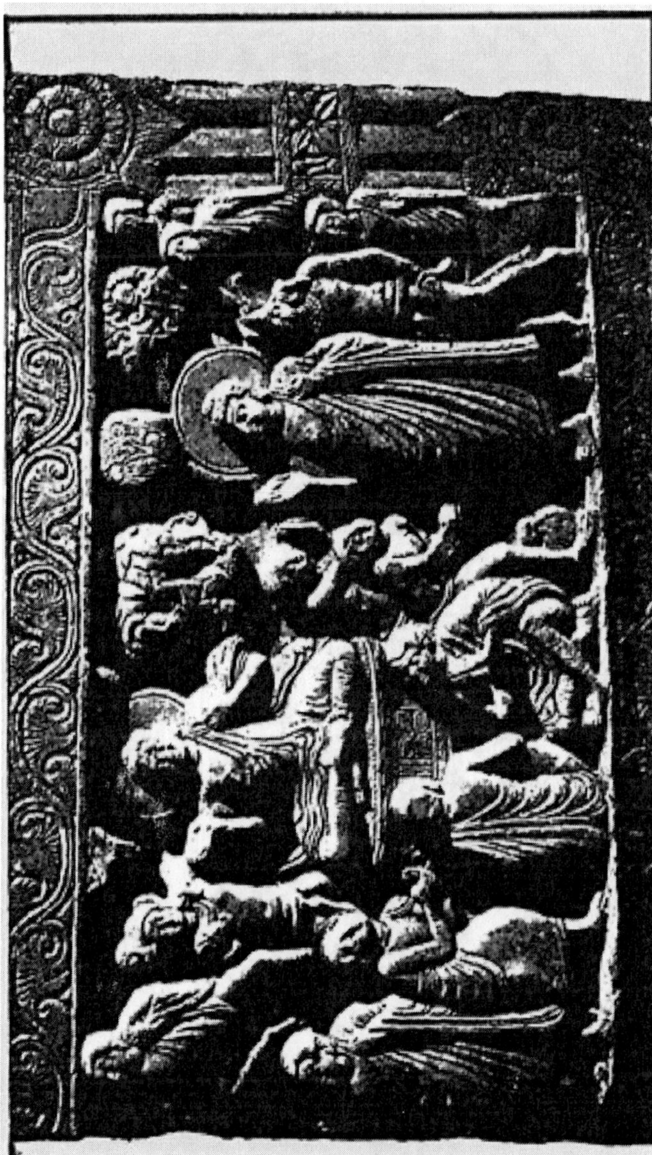

Pl. 18. The First Sermon in the Deer-Park at Benares, Nāgārjunikonda.

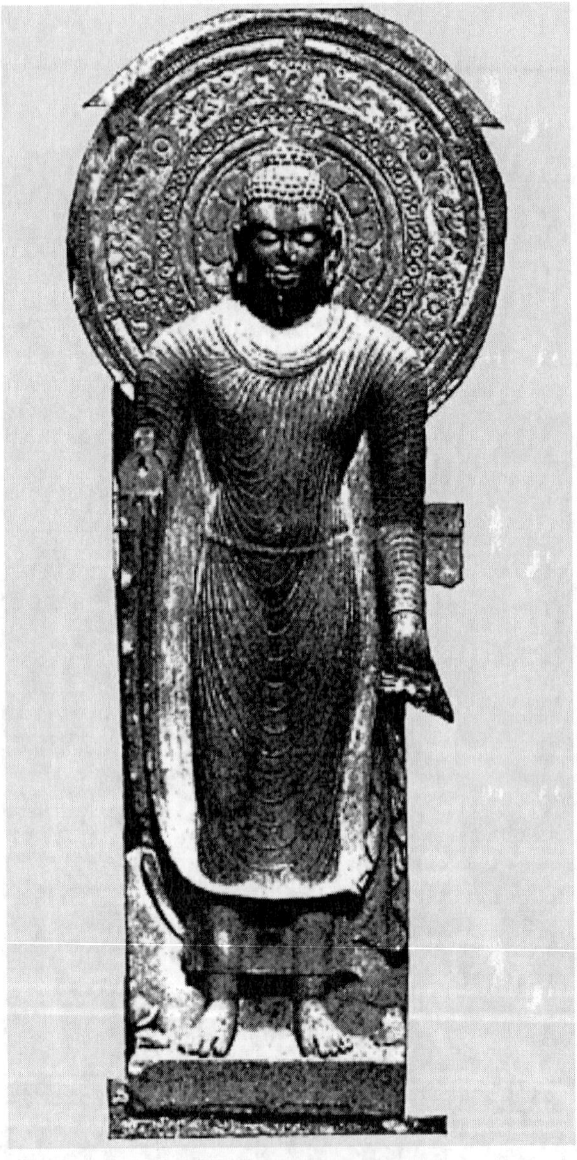

Pl. 19. Buddha Image of the Gupta period, Mathurā.
Curzon Museum, Mathurā.

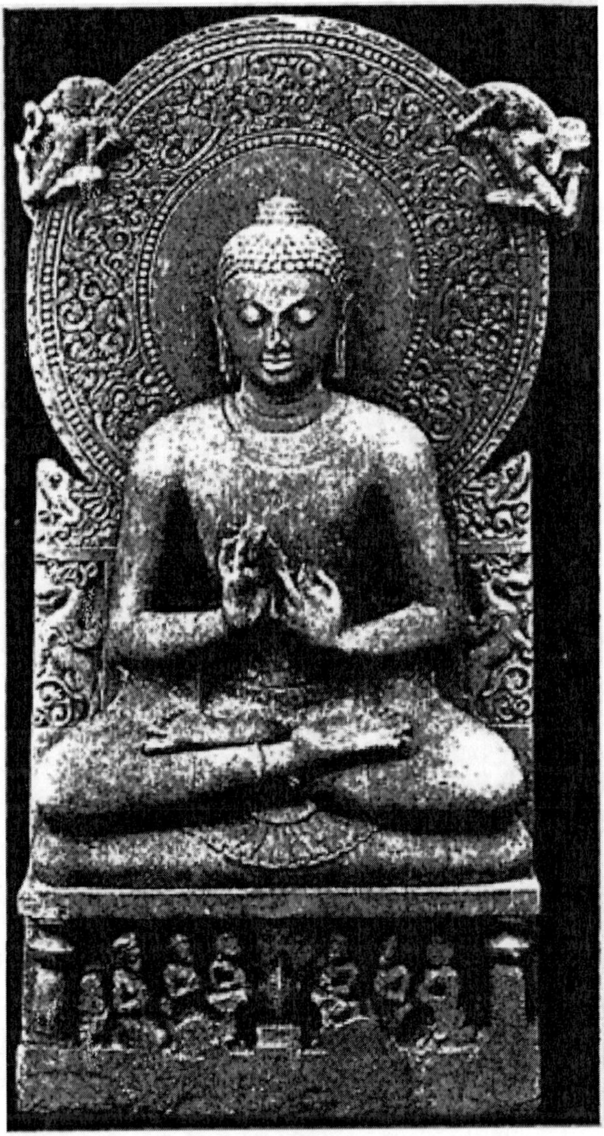

**Pl. 20. Preaching Buddha of the Gupta Period, Sārnāth.
Local Museum.**

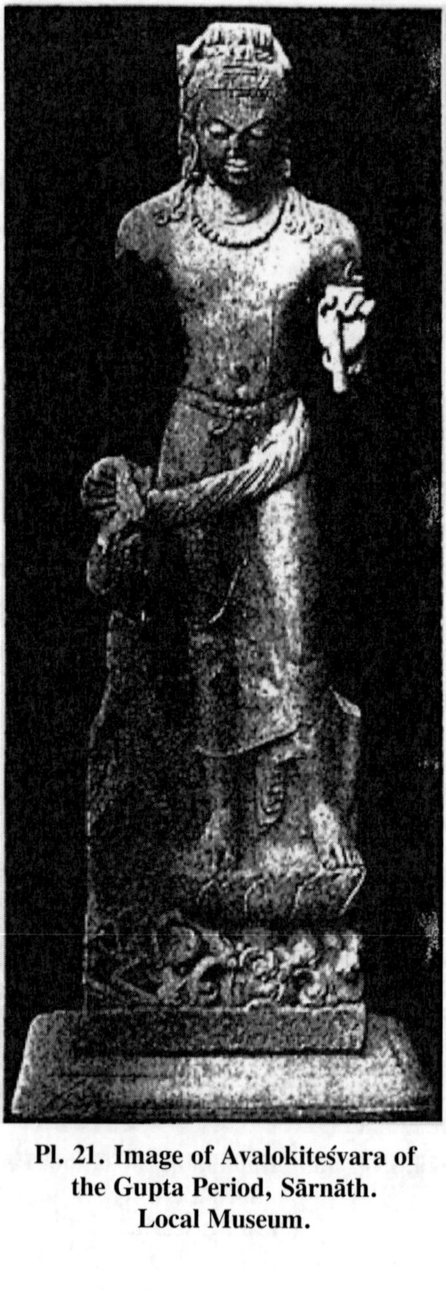

Pl. 21. Image of Avalokiteśvara of the Gupta Period, Sārnāth. Local Museum.

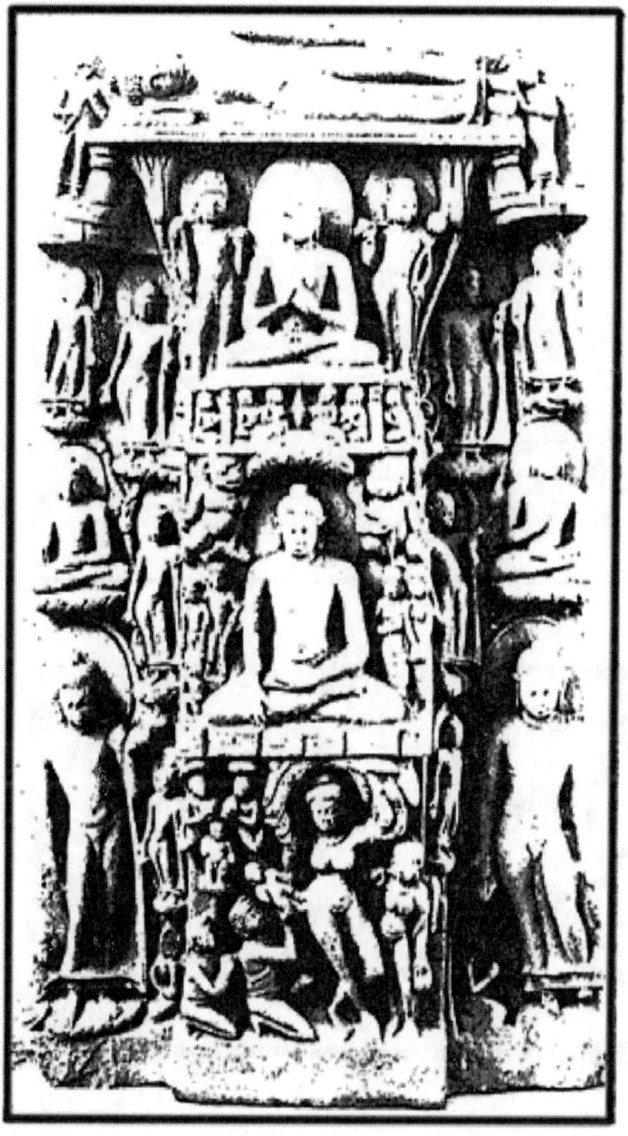

Pl. 22. Four Principal Moments of the Buddha Legend, on Stele from Sārnāth. Local Museum.

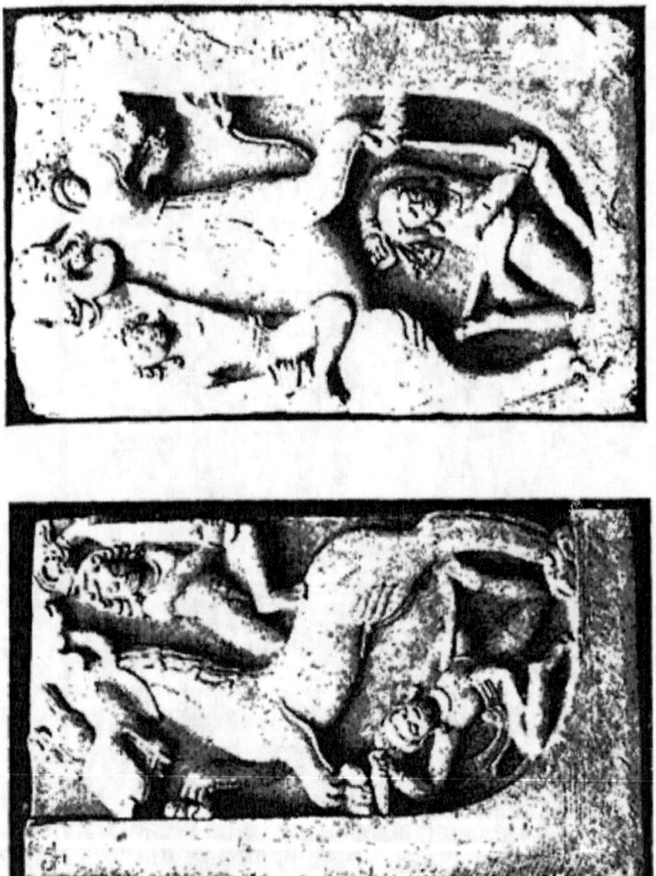

Pl. 23. Two Vyālakas from Sārnāth. Local Museum.

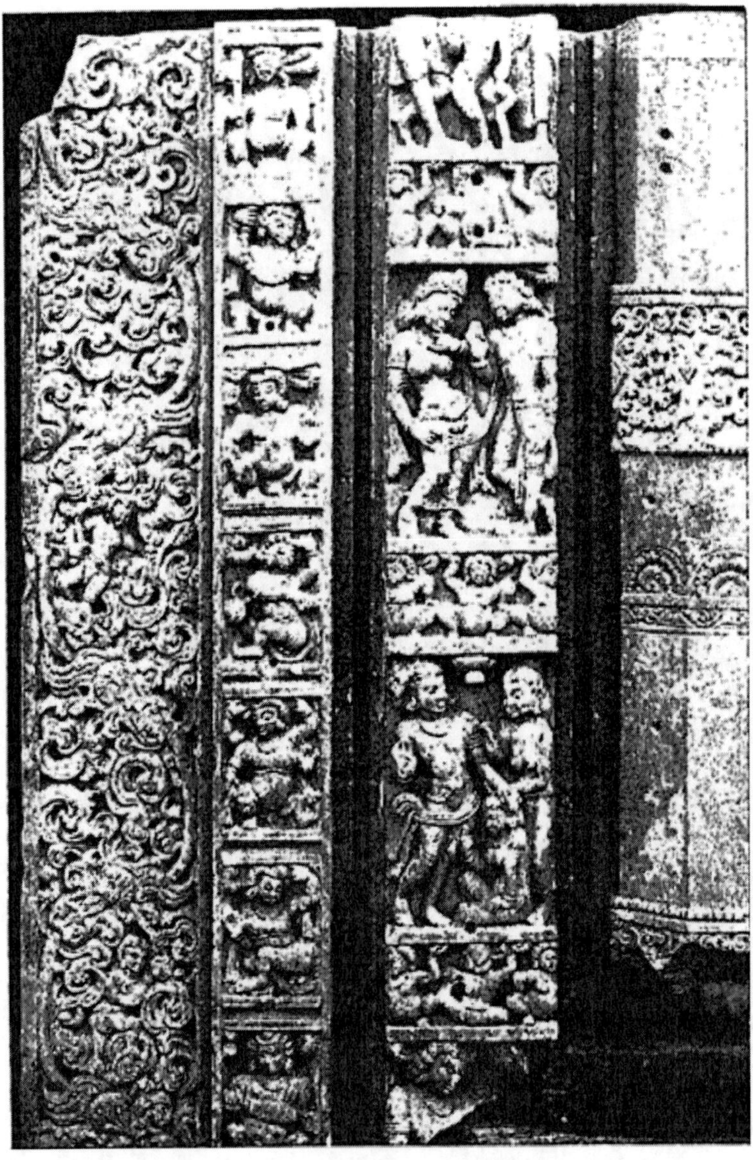

Pl. 24. Fragment showing Decorative Motifs, Sārnāth. Local Museum.

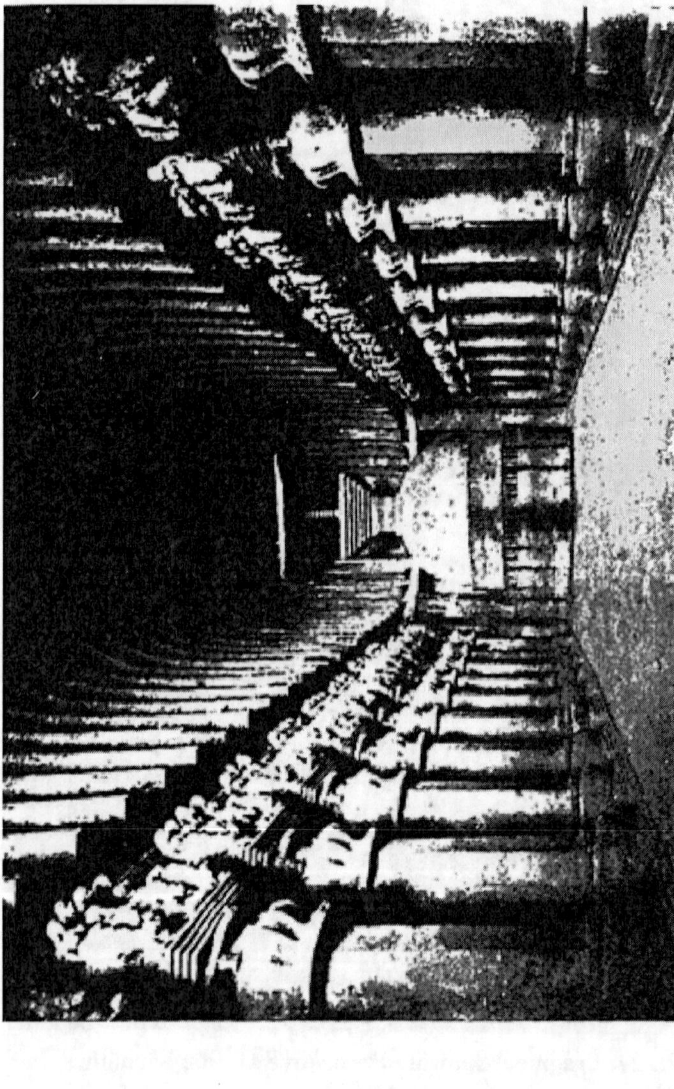

Pl. 25. Cave Temple, Kārli.

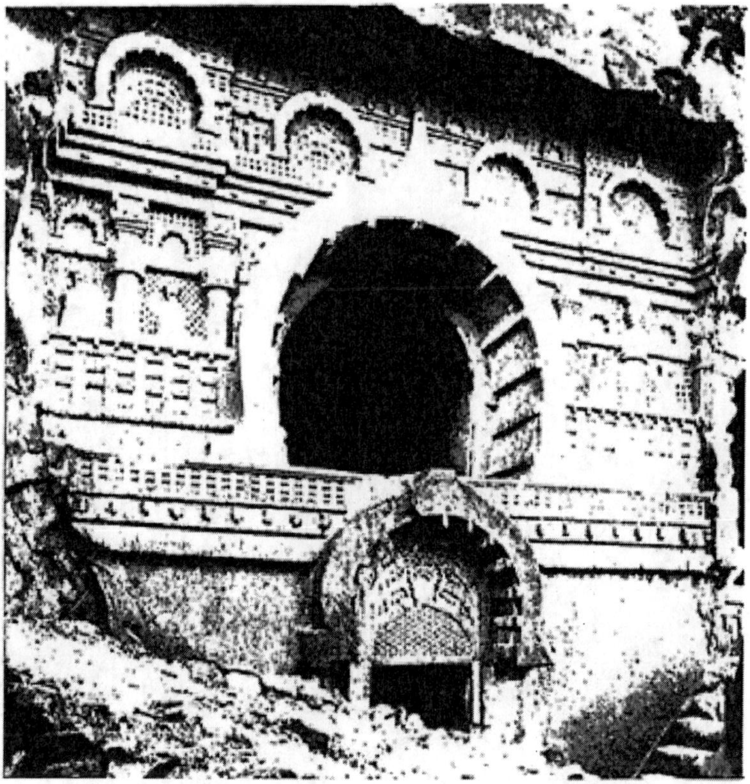

Pl. 26. Façade of Cave Temple, Nāsik. A.S.I.

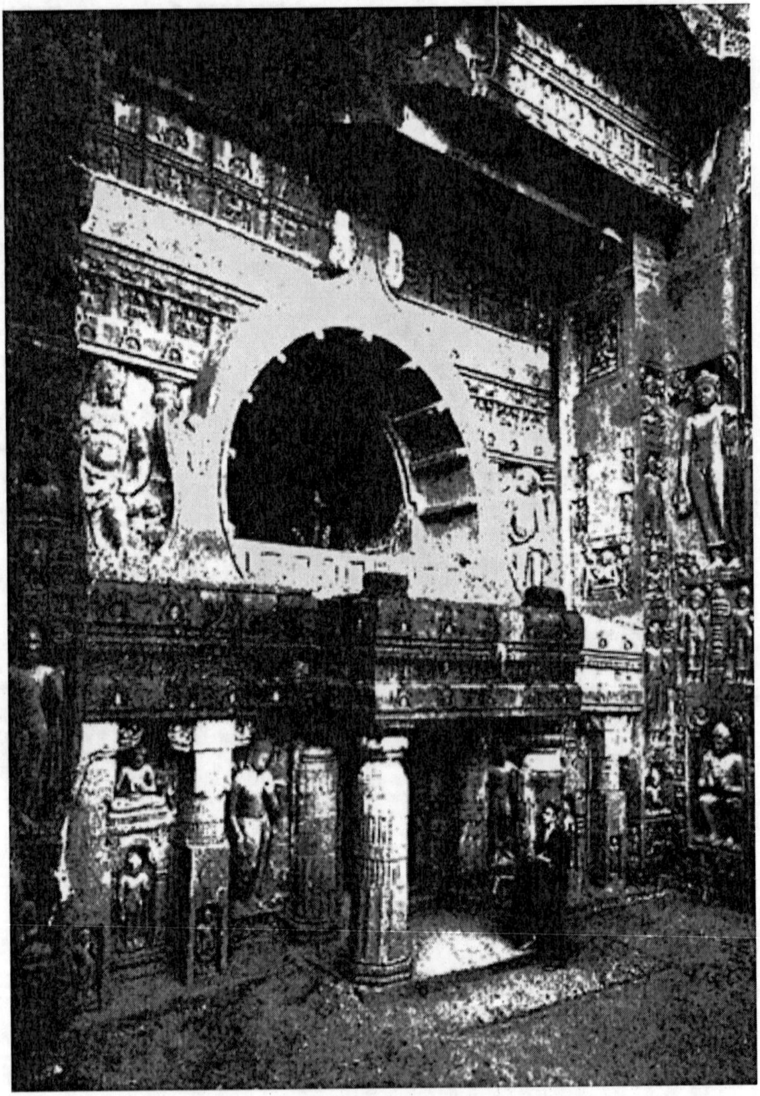

Pl. 27. Façade of Cave Temple, Ajānta.

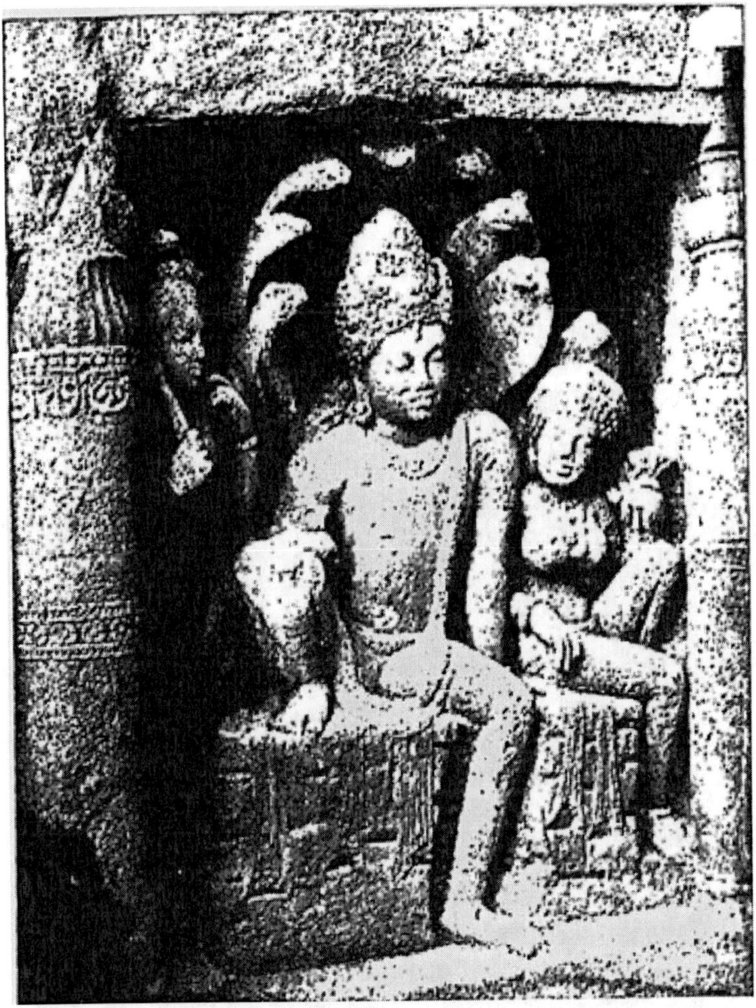

Pl. 28. Group of Nāgarāja and Nāgis, Ajānta.

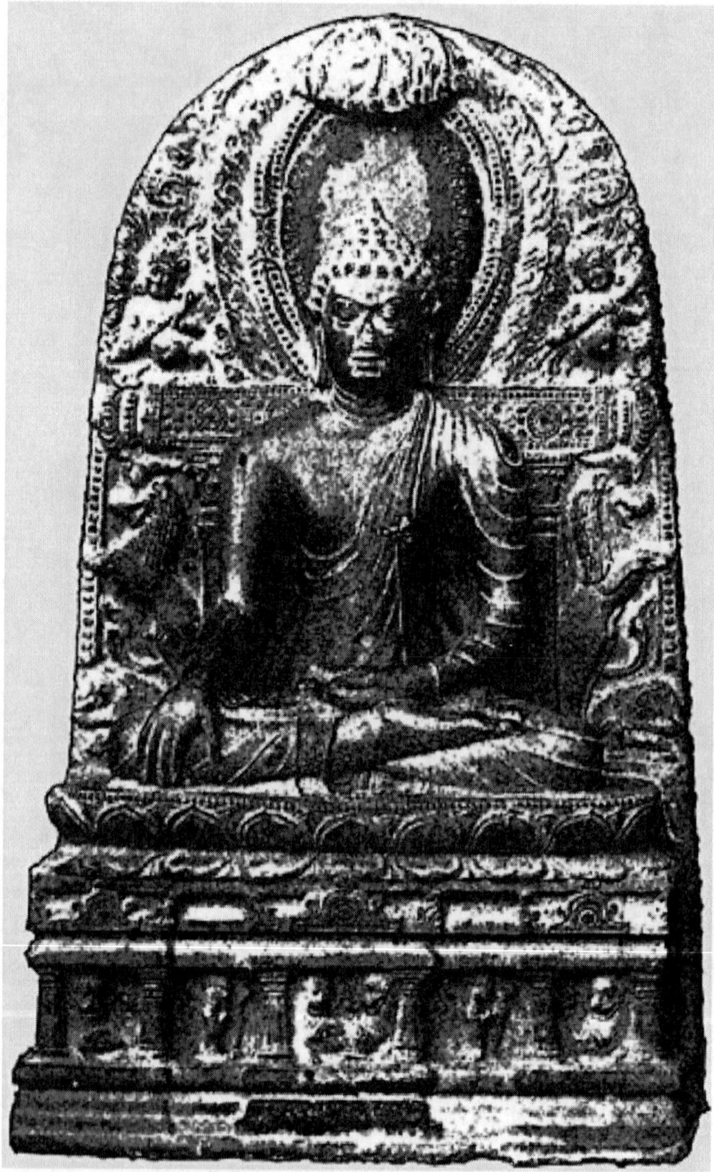

Pl. 29. Buddha Image from Kurkihār, S. Bihār. Provincial Museum, Lucknow.

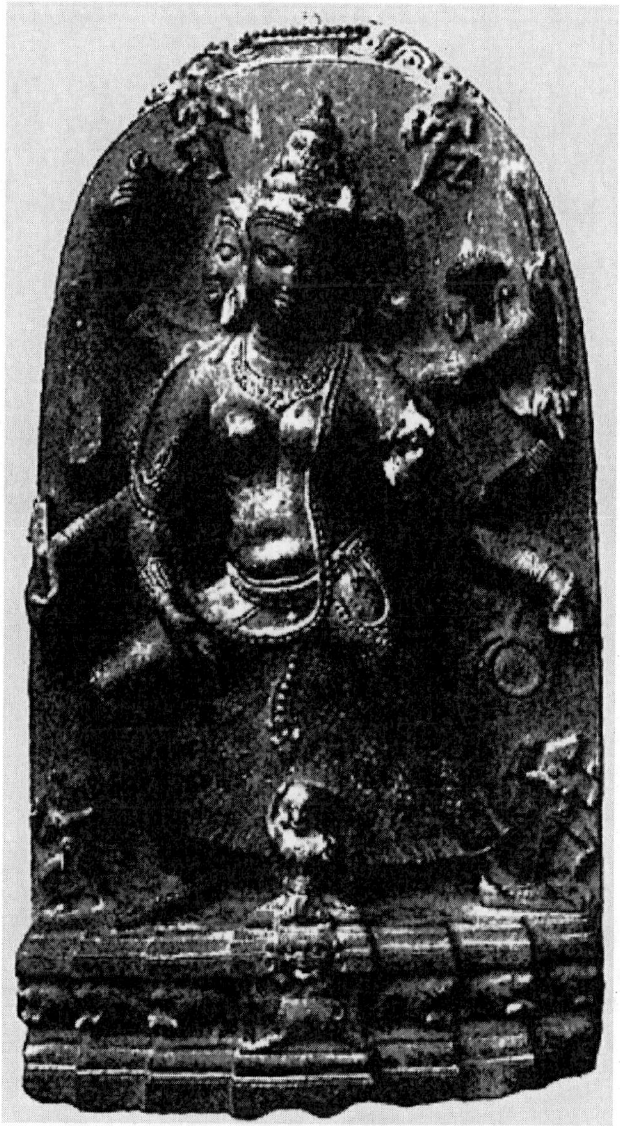

Pl. 30. Image of the Goddess Mārīchī from Kurkihār, S. Bihār. Provincial Museum, Lucknow.

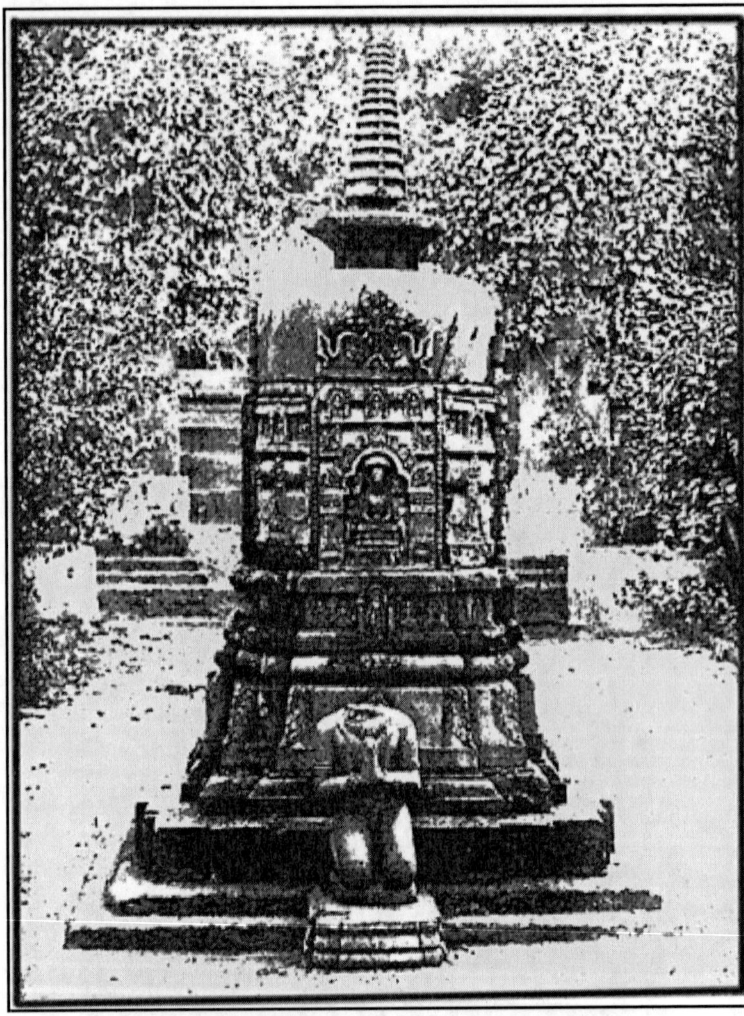

Pl. 31. Small-sized Stūpa in Temple Court, Bodh Gayā.

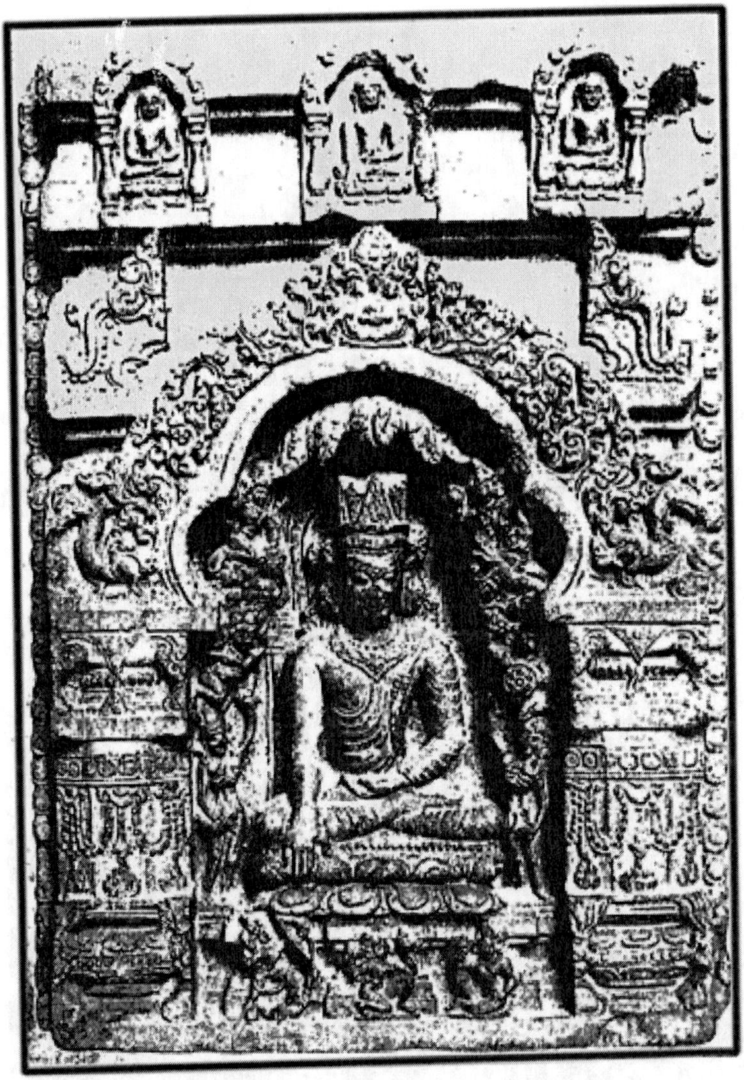

Pl. 32. Crowned Buddha from Bihār. Museum für Völkerkunde, Munich.

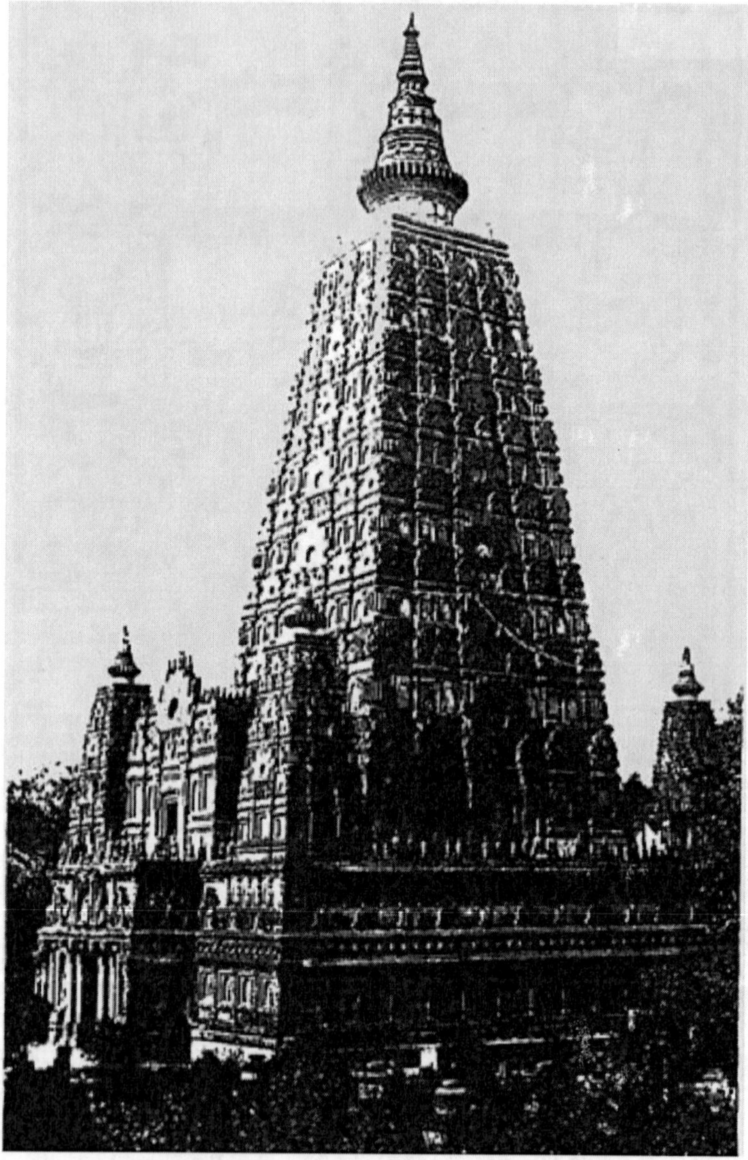

Pl. 33. Mahābodhi Temple, Bodh Gayā.

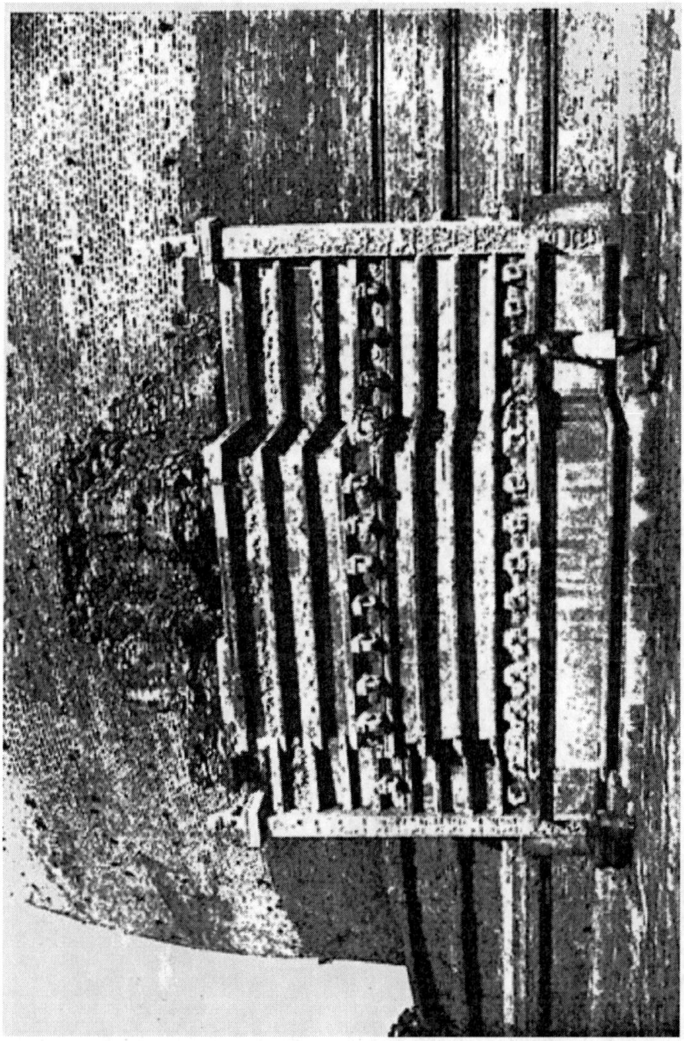

Pl. 34. Mirisavätiya Dāgaba, Anurādhapura, with Western Vāhalkada.

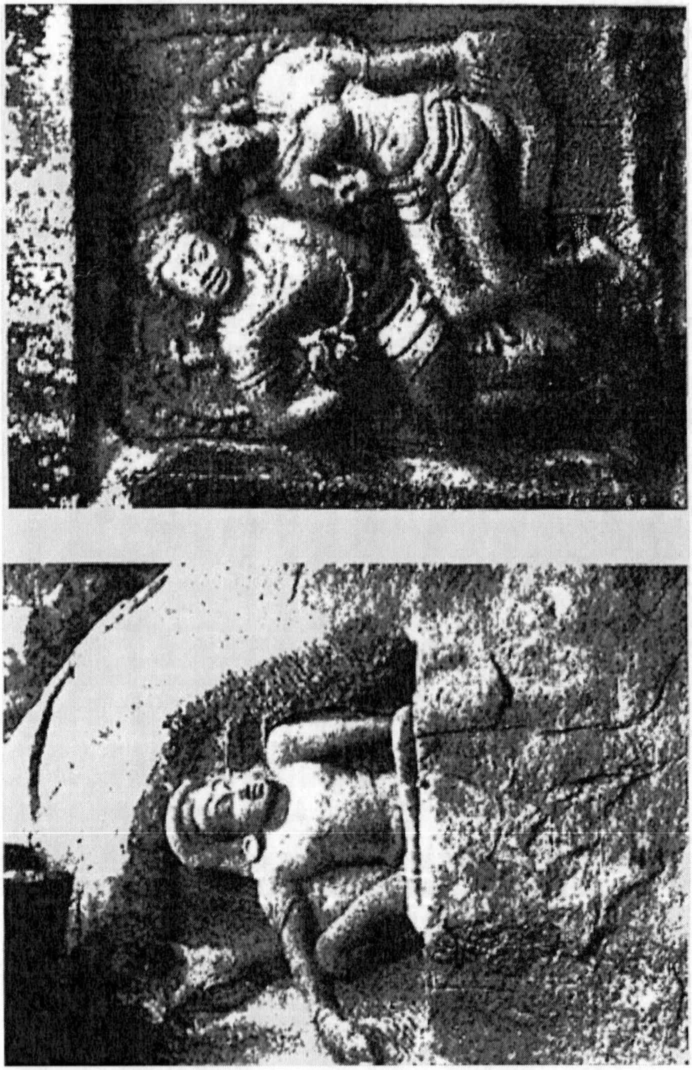

Pl. 35. Sculptures at Isurumuniya, Anurādhapura.

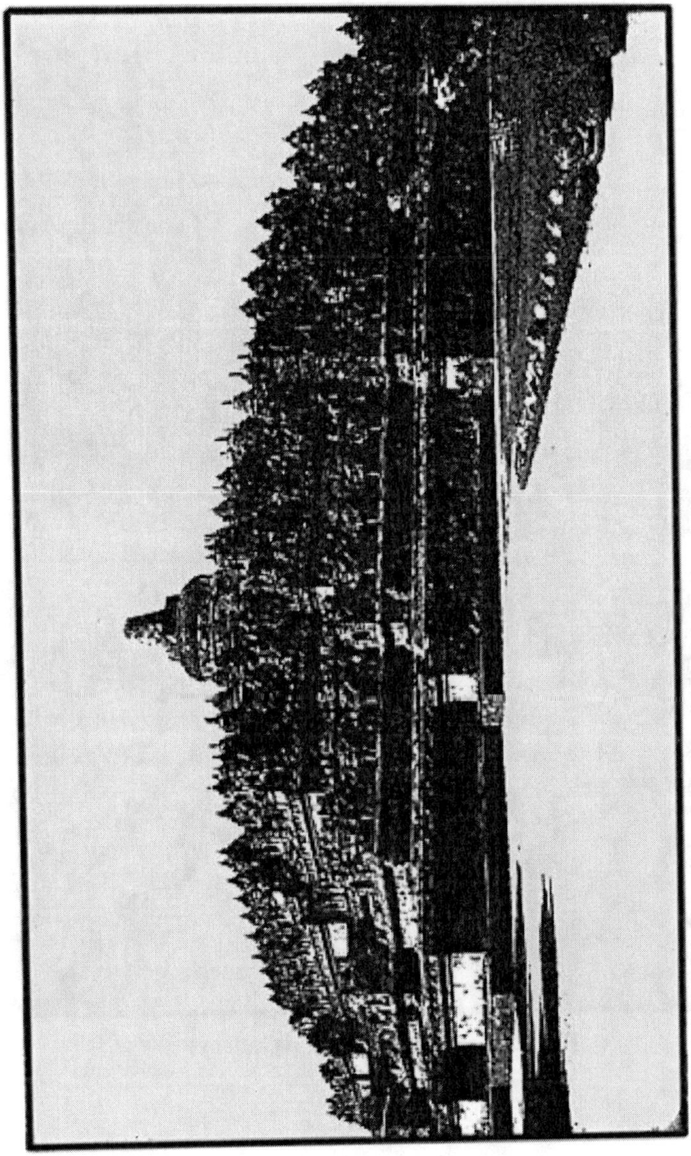

Pl. 36. View of Barabudur, after Restoration.

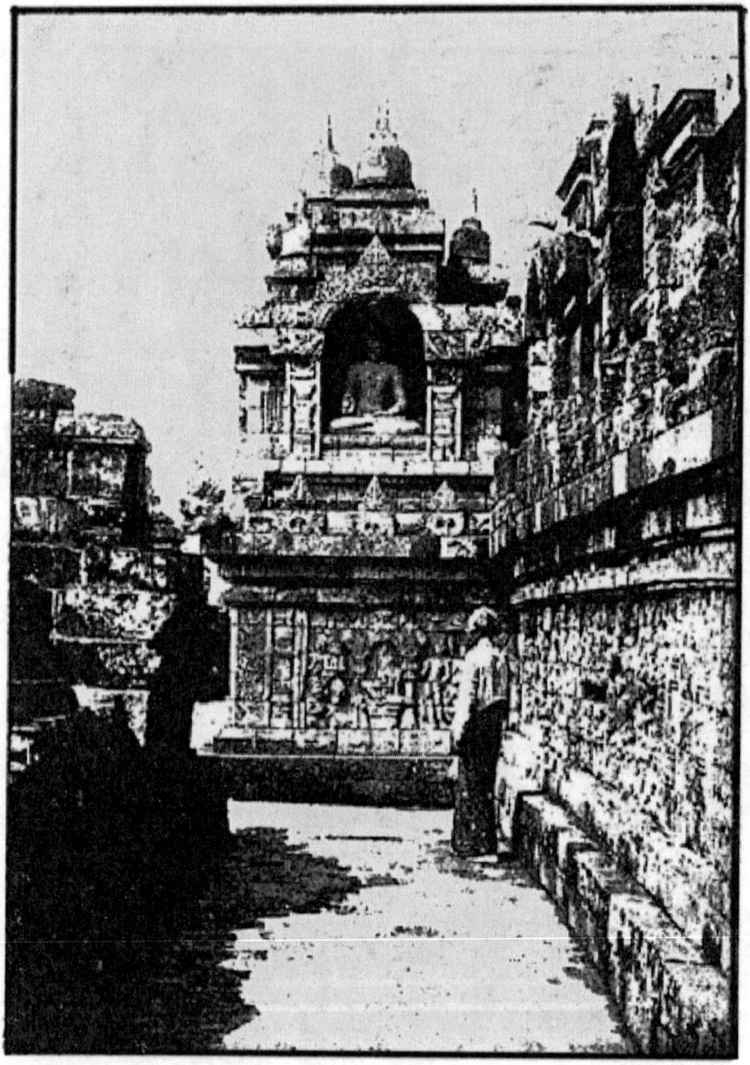

Pl. 37. Barabudur, Upper Gallery.

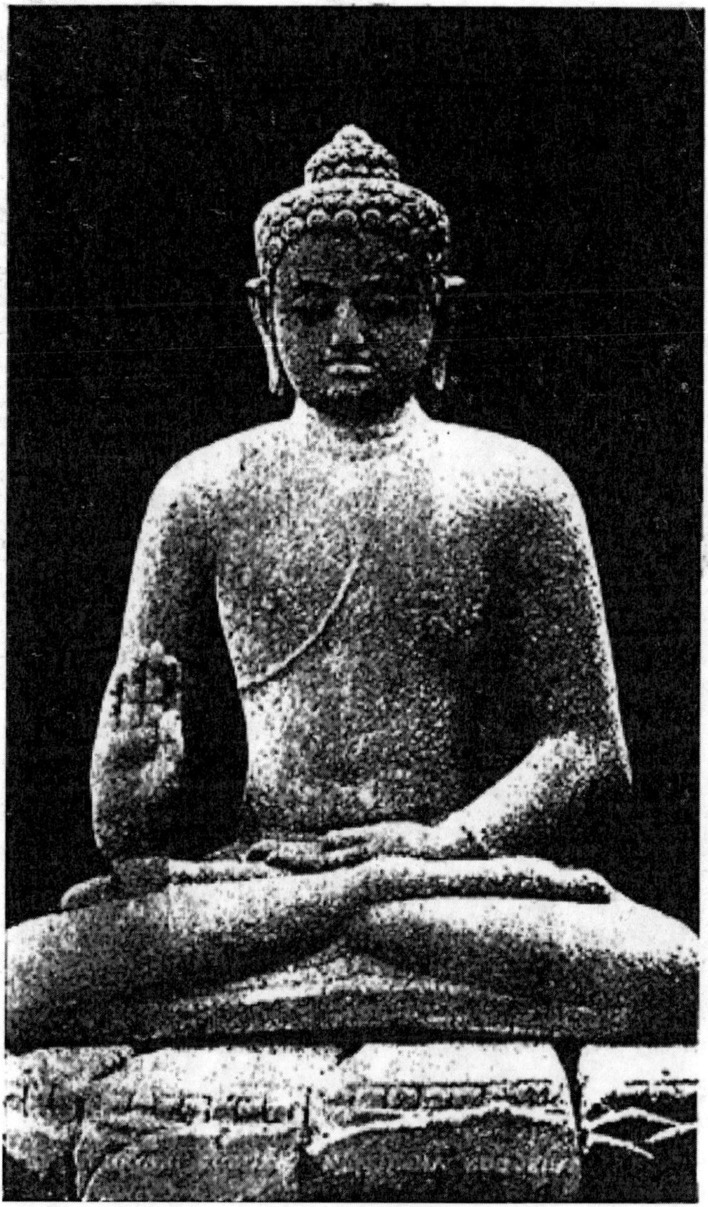

Pl. 38. Buddha Image.

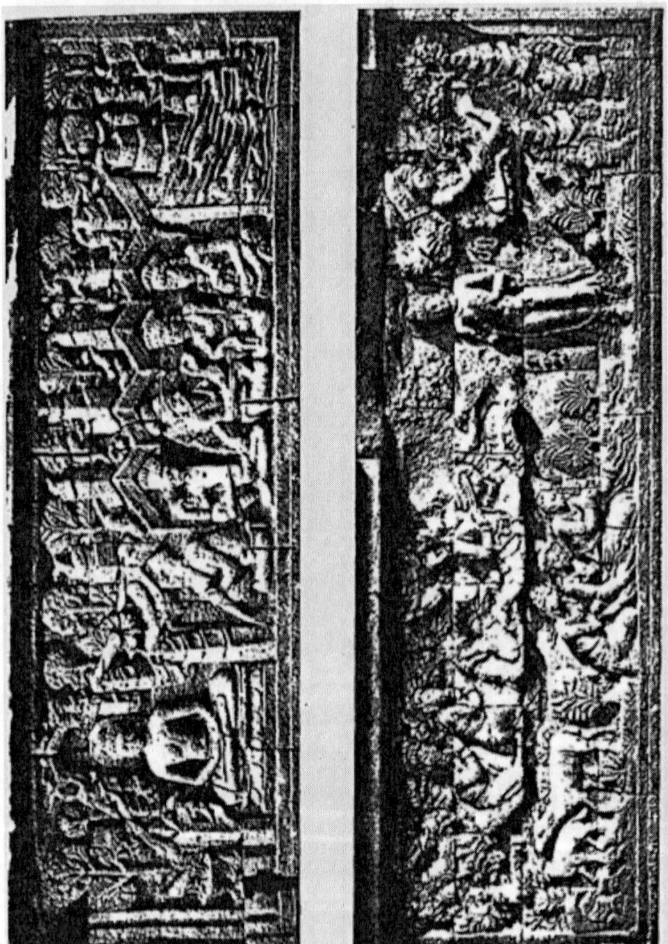

Pl. 39. a, b. Barabudur: Two scenes of the Buddha Legend.